"Fa   n-
all   i-
ti   d
ch

—Scot McKnight, professor of New Testament
at Northern Seminary and author of *A Church Called Tov*

"As parents, we can become overwhelmed by the conversation on race, not knowing where to turn and whose voices to trust. Helen Lee and Michelle Reyes are two leaders I know, trust, and respect. This book is a must-read for every parent seeking to learn, understand, and guide their families to engage in this critically important topic and time."

—Vivian Mabuni, speaker, author of *Open Hands, Willing Heart,*
and founder of *Someday Is Here* (podcast)

"In *The Race-Wise Family*, Helen Lee and Michelle Reyes relieve some of the pressure from adults who wonder where and how to lead their families in racial justice. This book is as tender as it is helpful. If families across the nation implemented even a fraction of what the authors suggest in *The Race-Wise Family*, we would see generational transformation."

—Jemar Tisby, PhD, *New York Times* bestselling
author of *The Color of Compromise* and *How to Fight Racism*

"Lee and Reyes are lovers of Jesus, people, and their families, and they offer a better way to help our children understand the complexities of racism and the hope we find in Scripture. With biblical clarity and practical advice, Lee and Reyes take the reader on a journey to a better place, whether the reader is from a minority or majority culture. Be encouraged rather than outraged, and be informed instead of being insulated. We can do better; this book will help."

—Ed Stetzer, executive director
of the Billy Graham Center at Wheaton College

"How I wish *The Race-Wise Family* was around in the early years of our multiracial church when people wanted a picturesque reconciliation that required no sacrifice. Thankfully, there is no expiration date for growth, even in these increasingly polarized times. Helen and Michelle do not gloss over the reality of race-based struggles and trauma, and I hold deep respect for the vulnerability they lend. *The Race-Wise Family* helps us name the barriers of fear, ignorance, apathy, and laziness that hinder us from growing and guiding the children in our lives. Helen and Michelle generously invite us to join them in actively building a generation of kingdom-minded children, families, churches, and communities. I believe this is a landmark work for our generation!"

—DORENA WILLIAMSON, author, bridge builder, and speaker

"Helen and Michelle have given parents and caregivers an amazing gift! Full of timely insight and practical wisdom, this book opens our imaginations to a holistic formation that will align our children (and the adults who love them) more closely with God's heart for righteousness and reconciliation."

—DAVID W. SWANSON, pastor and author of
Rediscipling the White Church

"This challenging and insightful resource offers helpful takeaways for every parent—every family—to do better."

—BRI STENSRUD, director of Women of Welcome

"What a timely resource for families to help them cut through all the rhetoric and arguments when it comes to loving one another! This book is a welcomed guide for dealing with one of the most divisive issues in our culture today."

—RUSTY GEORGE, lead pastor of Real Life Church
and author of *After Amen*

"Like you, I'm a parent who needs this book's clarifying definitions, memorable stories, and practical ideas to have better conversations and connections about race at home. *The Race-Wise Family* will help your family appreciate your ethnic past and others', navigate the tensions and opportunities of the present, and blaze a path of racial justice and reconciliation in the future."

—KARA POWELL, PHD, executive director of the Fuller Youth Institute
and co-author of *3 Big Questions That Change Every Teenager*

"This resource gives us a thoroughly biblical and profoundly practical tool to help form us and our kids into the image of the One who has laid down his life to tear down the dividing wall of hostility, so that we might be reconciled to God not in fragmented splinters but as one new humanity made whole. In a time when the topic of race can feel bewildering and complex, I am profoundly grateful for a resource that grounds us in a biblical approach to racial justice and reconciliation."
—ABRAHAM CHO, senior director of training for City to City NYC and North America

"*The Race-Wise Family* is full of actionable insights, sage counsel, and Christian warmth. Read it, talk about it with your children, and then embody these ten postures in your daily practice. You, your family, and your world will be better for it. Highly recommended!"
—TODD WILSON, PHD, co-founder and president of the Center for Pastor Theologians

"Now more than ever, we are exiting the path of cultural disconnect and social disharmony and, by faith, running the race toward collective consonance and understanding. Though you know the direction you want to go, you may be unsure about the steps that make up a successful practice. In these pages, Lee and Reyes offer a harness to support you on your way to becoming conduits of healing and hope."
—LUCRETIA BERRY, PHD, creator of Brownicity, educator, author, TED Speaker, and (in)courage contributor

"I've been waiting for this book for years. Lee and Reyes have crafted a deeply biblical, insightful, and practical book that I will use with my own children to help them understand their own multiethnicity in these complex and divided historic times."
—ROBERT ROMERO, JD, PHD, associate professor of Chicana/o and Central American studies; Asian American studies at UCLA

The Race-Wise Family

Ten Postures to Becoming Households of Healing and Hope

by Helen Lee and Michelle Ami Reyes

WATERBROOK

Details in some anecdotes and stories have been changed to protect the identities of the persons involved.

Grateful acknowledgment is made to the following for permission to use the material below:

Asian American Christian Collaborative: Excerpt from "Let's Talk About White Privilege and Slavery" by Michelle Reyes, published by the Asian American Christian Collaborative on June 22, 2020. (www.asianamericanchristiancollaborative.com/article/lets-talk-about-white-privilege-and-slavery). Used by permission of the Asian American Christian Collaborative.

Christianity Today: Excerpt from "Justice, Restoration & Wholeness in the Kingdom of God" by Michelle Ami Reyes, published on "The Better Samaritan Blog" by *Christianity Today* on March 12, 2021. (www.christianitytoday.com/better-samaritan/2021/march/justice-restoration-wholeness-in-kingdom-of-god.html). Used by permission of *Christianity Today*.

DaySpring Greeting Cards/(in)courage: Excerpt from *Courageous Joy: Delight in God Through Every Season (An (in)Courage Bible Study)* by Michelle Reyes, copyright © 2021 by DaySpring Cards, Inc. (Grand Rapids, MI: Revell, a division of Baker Publishing Group, 2021); adapted excerpts from "Finding Safe Spaces in the Midst of Racism" by Michelle Reyes, published by on April 17, 2020. (www.incourage.me/2020/04/finding-safe-spaces-in-the-midst-of-racism.html). Used by permission of DaySpring Greeting Cards/(in)courage.

Library of Congress Cataloging-in-Publication Data
Names: Lee, Helen, author. | Reyes, Michelle Ami, author.
Title: The race-wise family : ten postures to becoming households of healing and hope / by Helen Lee and Michelle Reyes.
Description: First edition. | Colorado Springs : WaterBrook, [2022] | Includes bibliographical references.
Identifiers: LCCN 2021043898 | ISBN 9780593193952 (paperback) | ISBN 9780593193969 (ebook)
Subjects: LCSH: Parenting—Religious aspects—Christianity. | Child rearing—Religious aspects—Christianity. | Race—Religious aspects—Christianity. | Racism—Religious aspects—Christianity. | Race relations—Religious aspects—Christianity.
Classification: LCC BV4529 .L435 2022 | DDC 248.8/45—dc23
LC record available at https://lccn.loc.gov/2021043898

Printed in the United States of America on acid-free paper

waterbrookmultnomah.com

1 2 3 4 5 6 7 8 9

First Edition

Interior book design by Edwin Vazquez.

SPECIAL SALES Most WaterBrook books are available at special quantity discounts when purchased in bulk by corporations, organizations, and special-interest groups. Custom imprinting or excerpting can also be done to fit special needs. For information, please email specialmarketscms@penguinrandomhouse.com.

To every mother and father longing to make a difference,
may your family and your children be the keys to bringing
hope and healing in our racially broken world

Foreword

My wife, Vicki, loves maps. I learned of this love when we started dating in 1990. We met my freshman year of college and have been together ever since. For thirty years, we have loved each other as husband and wife. And for thirty years, I have beheld her fondness for maps! When I say she loves maps, I mean the old-school paper maps, the kind you unfold like an ancient scroll. Only recently has she reluctantly embraced digital maps.

Why does Vicki love maps? Because they are guides that get us to our destination. With a map in her hand, we have driven across America, discovering things we had never seen or experienced before.

But every map must come from people—cartographers— who have gone before us and recorded the details so we can arrive at our destinations. Helen Lee and Michelle Reyes are two such people. Like skilled travel guides, they take us to a new place of grace, where King Jesus is "creating in himself one new people" (Ephesians 2:15, NLT) that is wonderfully composed of a blood-purchased people from "every tribe and language and people and nation" (Revelation 5:9, NLT). God is building his redeemed, colorful, and multiethnic family. Sacred Scripture says it this way:

> This is God's plan: Both Gentiles and Jews who believe the Good News share equally in the riches inherited by God's children. Both are part of the same body, and both enjoy the promise of blessings because they belong to Christ Jesus. (Ephesians 3:6, NLT)

This new, multicolored family is called the church. As God's family loves one another across ethnic, class, and gender barriers, we bear witness to Jesus, his gospel, and his kingdom (Galatians 3:27–29).

You are in good hands with your mapmakers. Helen is an accomplished author, publishing veteran, theologian, and practitioner of racial reconciliation. Her words flow not just from a prolific pen but from a life that embodies what she teaches. Michelle is an activist; she has done the heavy lifting, along with her husband, of planting a multiethnic church in East Austin, Texas. And she is a well-respected author. She, too, writes out of a life that is immersed in the reality of the book you hold in your hands.

These two godly, gifted, intelligent women have provided us with a map called *The Race-Wise Family: Ten Postures to Becoming Households of Healing and Hope*. I envision thousands of households and Bible studies reading *The Race-Wise Family*, being inspired, challenged, and equipped with practical tools to become agents of gospel-shaped racial reconciliation.

Discipleship begins in the home, with parents beholding the greatness of Jesus, living in allegiance to Jesus, and calling their children, primarily through an embodied faith, to follow Jesus. Helen and Michelle write, "Standing against racial injustice is part of our Christian witness, but if our children are driven more by a desire to conform to the cultural moment than by kingdom-minded values, they won't have the wisdom to do what is right even when it is unpopular to do so."

Helen and Michelle, thank you. You have given us a map worth following.

DR. DERWIN L. GRAY
cofounder and lead pastor of Transformation Church,
a multiethnic, multigenerational community, and author
of *How to Heal Our Racial Divide: What the Bible Says,
and the First Christians Knew, About Racial Reconciliation*

Contents

Foreword   ix

Authors' Note   xv

Introduction   xix

     Posture One: **Valuing Multiethnicity**   3

     Posture Two: **Seeing Color**   16

     Posture Three: **Understanding a Biblical View of Racism**   29

     Posture Four: **Opening Our Hearts to Lament**   44

     Posture Five: **Speaking Words of Love and Truth**   61

     Posture Six: **Responding to Current Events**   73

     Posture Seven: **Addressing Privilege**   87

     Posture Eight: **Assessing Our Biases**   104

     Posture Nine: **Journeying Toward Racial Healing**   120

     Posture Ten: **Raising Kingdom-Minded Children**   133

Epilogue   147

Acknowledgments   151

Appendix 1: **The Multiethnicity Quotient Assessment**   155

Appendix 2: **Kid-Friendly Definitions**   161

Appendix 3: **Media Suggestions for a Race-Wise Family**   165

Appendix 4: **Prayers for a Race-Wise Family**   177

Appendix 5: **Recommendations for Future Learning for Parents**   179

Notes   181

Authors' Note

PARENTS ACROSS THE COUNTRY are wrestling with how to talk about race right now. Though issues of race and racism have always existed, viral videos and a flow of newsworthy incidents have forced all of us to come face to face with police brutality, anti-Asian hate crimes, systemic injustice, national protests, and more. Even if we have tried to shield our children from breaking news and upsetting images, our kids are still overhearing conversations at school and on social media, and they are looking for guidance. Addressing race and racism in the home is no longer something we parents can avoid.

Undoubtedly, addressing issues of race feels daunting. What if we say the wrong thing? Where do we even begin a conversation on something as big and heavy as racism? How should we respond to our children's questions about events happening in the news? What if they ask what protest they should go to? How often should we talk about race with our kids anyway? What is age appropriate and what is not?

This book is a road map for addressing race in your home. We're here to equip you with a biblical foundation for how to raise race-wise children for both the present and the future.

And who are "we"? Although we wish we could talk with you face to face over a cup of chai or coffee, for the present moment allow us to introduce ourselves.

I (Helen) am the mom of three teenage boys. They along with my husband and me comprise a monoethnic but multicultural family: 100 percent Korean by blood but a mixture of Canadian and American by citizenship. Having been married to a Canadian for nearly thirty years, I can tell you that there are vast cultural differences between growing up Canadian and growing up American! I'm also a longtime Christian publishing professional and a public communicator who has written and spoken about race and ethnicity for decades. (You can find a chapter about this topic in my first book, *The Missional Mom*.)

I (Michelle) am a second-generation Indian American married to Aaron, a second-generation Mexican American. Together we planted Hope Community Church, a minority-led multicultural church in Austin, Texas, where I also serve as a scholar in residence. We live in a disadvantaged Black and Brown community, and our everyday vocational ministry involves crossing cultures and navigating heavy issues such as immigration, gun violence, racial profiling, police brutality, homelessness, and more. In addition, I serve as the vice president of the Asian American Christian Collaborative (AACC), and I am the author of *Becoming All Things: How Small Changes Lead to Lasting Connections Across Cultures*. I regularly write and speak on issues of race, culture, justice, and faith. Aaron and I are raising two young children to know that living out the gospel means loving *all* our neighbors and caring for both their spiritual and their physical needs.

In this book, we invite you to join us in the messy, wild journey of raising kingdom-minded children who love God and love their neighbors with all their hearts, minds, and bodies. In the pages that follow, you'll learn about our own stories and how they have had an impact on our understanding of race, specifically as Asian American Christian women. We're also going to lay down a foundation of biblical theology on race and suggest practical family activities and conversation starters for you to pursue with your children.

We don't think anyone ever arrives at perfect knowledge in this area. But with a spirit of humility because we still have a long way to go in our own understanding, we strive to have the posture of lifelong learners, extending grace to both others and ourselves when errors occur—which will happen! We're on a journey together now, and we hope and pray that our words will inspire you and equip you for the road ahead.

Introduction

What Does It Mean to Be Race-Wise?

So, WHAT DOES it mean to be race-wise?[1] We need wisdom to make good choices as we navigate the topic of race, a topic that is fraught with potential misunderstanding, divisiveness, and pain. Being a race-wise family means asking God for help in unpacking racial issues and seeking his direction to know how to identify and combat racism in all its overt and subtle forms. This is holistic spiritual work that requires both orthodoxy (right thinking) and orthopraxy (right living). In other words, the goal of a race-wise family is not simply to grow in intellectual understanding of the Bible's discussions about race and culture but rather to pursue a biblical vision of human flourishing in the home, the community, and the nation. By the time you finish this book, you will be able to see the richness, beauty, and depth of God's intent for people of every ethnicity, culture, and language to flourish together as well as how this vision should affect your family's daily conversations and routines.

Parents bear the responsibility of teaching and training their children. We can't assume that our kids are learning all they need to know from other sources, even good sources such as their schools or churches. We have a unique calling to disci-

> The goal of a race-wise family is not simply to grow in intellectual understanding of the Bible's discussions about race and culture but rather to pursue a biblical vision of human flourishing in the home, the community, and the nation.

ple our children, and we have to take ownership of teaching our kids about race from a biblical perspective. Our society is swimming in cultural myths and fallacies, and our children are consuming messages without even realizing it. If they're not being informed and equipped in the home, you can be sure their views are being formed elsewhere. In fact, we don't always know what kinds of messages our children are receiving from the cultural influences around them until something happens that exposes the gaps in their knowledge—as well as our own.

For example, when my (Helen's) eldest son, Jason, was twelve years old and on a new Little League baseball team, he heard words from a teammate that took him by surprise. "Ching-chong, ching-chong!" came the taunt from a white tween named Dylan while another white teammate howled with laughter beside him. The boys then went a step further and took their taunts to Instagram, posting the same phrase on Jason's page, which I was able to immortalize in a screenshot. I then sent it to the coach. Soon after, the boys were suspended for two games.

At the game after the suspension, Dylan's mom approached me and introduced herself. "I just wanted to reach out to you and apologize for Dylan's behavior. And I want to thank you for letting me know about that incident. I was completely shocked. I want you to know that we have told him that it is absolutely unacceptable for him to say those words." She shook her head as if still in disbelief. "I had no idea my son could ever do such a thing. I am so embarrassed."

Dylan was clearly learning about race somewhere, enough that he could speak racialized language to one of his teammates of color, but until this incident, his parents weren't even aware of what their son had absorbed over the years.

Of course, this incident raises questions. How can we teach and train our children in the area of racial understanding when our own education may be limited? Most of us aren't scholars in the subject. In fact, some of us might still be at the beginning of our own journeys of understanding issues of race and culture. How exactly do you talk to your children about an innocent Black man who suffocated to death at the hands of the police? How do you explain to your children that they can't go with you to the grocery store because our country is being openly hostile to people who look like your family? How do you navigate situations in which relatives or neighbors are spouting racist rhetoric at your dinner table while your children are sitting there, soaking it all in? How do you teach your kids which words are appropriate and which words aren't? What do you say after someone accuses you of being a racist? Issues of race have touched us all, but that doesn't mean we're automatically equipped to properly respond.

Part of the challenge for Christian parents is that we don't have a good understanding of what the goal really is in the area of racial reconciliation. Plain and simple, we don't have a unified biblical perspective on issues of race. Much of the church hasn't provided good teaching in this area either. If anything, we are seeing the exact opposite dynamic—that racial issues not only divide people of different ethnic backgrounds but also drive wedges between members of the body of Christ. The fact that most of us didn't have these types of conversations or lifestyles modeled to us when we were kids ourselves has left us underprepared and uneducated while our nation continues to struggle in this area and the church alongside it.

Perhaps you were taught that Christians are supposed to be color-blind. Maybe issues of race were never discussed in your home while you were growing up, and you didn't even think about the color of your skin until recently. Maybe you come from a culture in which you were taught to just stay quiet, keep your head down, and not make a big deal about the racism you experience. Or perhaps you were taught that issues of race are too political and divisive and that Christians aren't supposed to weigh in on these conversations because we're supposed to just focus on the gospel.

Perhaps you're a parent of color navigating your own experiences of racial pain and trauma. It's hard to equip and empower our kids when we're carrying our own hurt. When my (Michelle's) eldest child, Akash, started school and became both aware of and curious about race, his questions opened floodgates of shame and grief from my own childhood. I had memories of eating alone in the school cafeteria because, as my classmates told me, they didn't want to be near my "smelly" food. There were also the dehumanizing comments about my brown skin. I didn't realize how much I had been holding in about my past until my son wanted to talk about different skin colors, ethnic roots, and more. Many parents of color hope that the hostilities directed toward them as children are nothing more than distant memories, but I quickly realized that I had to find healing in order to prepare my children for the hostile realities of race and to guide them into a more resilient future.

Regardless of the reason you're reading this book, in our increasingly diversified and still-divided country, we can't afford to create color-blind homes or simply avoid racially charged cultural moments for fear of doing things wrong. The witness of the church is at stake; the integrity of the gospel is weakened every time Christians battle over issues of race rather than unify around the call to reconciliation that we believe is clear in Scripture. More than that, if we don't choose to be race-wise families, we will miss out on discipling our kids holistically. If we and our children aren't intentionally working toward dismantling racism in our country, we're actually making the problems and divisions of race worse. Either we're working toward healing and hope, or we're participating in the very problems that are tearing this country apart; there's no such thing as nonengagement with race.

Nevertheless, that doesn't mean that if we intentionally pursue greater racial understanding and advocacy, everything will go smoothly. Perhaps to dispel some fears, we want to make it clear up front: you will make mistakes. (We certainly still do too.) You won't always get it right. You'll find yourself in situations where you don't have the best words to discuss issues of race with your kids, or you might even feel like you failed to model a biblical response to a race-related incident. Making mistakes and learning from them is part of the process.

The goal of this journey is not perfection but rather the *posture* of a race-wise heart and a desire to learn to grow. In *The Race-Wise Family*, we suggest ten postures that Christian parents can pursue to begin shaping their lives and their families into beacons of hope and healing to those around them. There is no way to catalog an appropriate Christian response to every race-related incident. Each one is unique, and there is no easy catchall solution that addresses every situation you or your kids may encounter. But by pursuing these postures, you will grow in your understanding in this area and be better equipped to handle racial issues. All that is required is your willingness to dive in, learn, and keep pursuing these postures even when you experience failures and setbacks, as we all do.

We also want to offer a special word to parents of color on healing from racial trauma (see posture 9). As women of color, we know the realities of racial trauma firsthand, and we also know that part of the way to find healing is to cultivate a safe space to address the particular pains and challenges we have experienced. However, we encourage everyone to read this chapter because we believe it's helpful for all parents to understand the challenges that exist for families of color.

Our deep desire is to help parents learn how to both train their children and transform their families into race-wise households. We are here to help you see and engage with the realities of race all around us and to do so from a biblical foundation. Our hope and prayer is that God will use our words to direct the posture of your family's hearts so that you and your children will feel equipped to understand current dialogues about race and to embody a Spirit-led response that resonates with God's clear heart for all his image bearers.

This is an opportunity for us parents to make changes that can have a lasting impact on us, our children, and, by extension, our communities, churches, and nation. It might feel impossible to alter the views and actions of our society such that racial issues disappear, but we can begin with small steps in our homes as we raise our children to treat all people equally and respectfully. By reading this book, you are taking the first step toward the biblical vision of true healing, peace, and flourishing for people of all ethnicities.

The Race-Wise Family

Valuing Multiethnicity

I (HELEN) REMEMBER a morning when I was teaching in my church's Sunday school program. My class of kindergarteners through fifth graders was majority white, with my youngest the only person of Asian descent at the table, and I was leading the kids through an exercise in understanding their ethnic roots. When it was my son's turn to share about his connection to Korea, one of the other children interjected, "That's the same as China, right?"

"No, Korea is a different country," I explained.

"China, Korea—whatever. It's all the same," he said.

In his third-grade understanding, the word *Asian* had come to represent a variety of ethnic groups without distinction. It was also clear that he didn't place value on identifying the differences between Korea and China. I had to patiently help him see that these were two distinct countries and people groups with their own identities and cultures. I knew the boy's parents, both of whom were well educated and culturally sensitive, but this was a detail of multiethnic understanding that had apparently never been covered in their home. If there hadn't been a Sunday school teacher who herself was the daughter of Korean immigrants, this young child may never have learned that day that China and Korea aren't at all the same.

When the Bible refers to people of "every nation, tribe, people and language" (Revelation 7:9), it is acknowledging details about God's intentionally created humanity that many Christians still might be overlooking. We live in a beautifully diverse world, and the biblical understanding of multiethnicity is foundational to becoming race-wise Christians. Often ignorance, discrimination, and ethnic or racial hatred come down to simply not valuing multiethnic voices and experiences.

In this chapter, we'll take a deeper dive into what multiethnicity means, why it matters (especially within the body of Christ), and how families can play a special role in reflecting this value. We have chosen the word *multiethnicity* intentionally because valuing multiethnicity is a biblical principle, one that reflects the heart of God toward his people, seen first in his selection of a particular ethnic group—the Israelites—and seen now in his open arms to people of all ethnic backgrounds, who are given the opportunity through God's grace and mercy to be adopted into his spiritual family (Galatians 3:26–29).

We also want to clarify that multiethnicity in and of itself isn't the goal. While Revelation 7 presents a complete vision of the redeemed in its glorious diversity—unified in a posture of worship—the focus of the celebration is our God in the highest, and knowing him is our chief goal. In other words, pursuing multiethnicity is an extension of our worship of God. Nevertheless, throughout Scripture, God clearly acknowledges and values diversity, both for his own pleasure and for the spread of the gospel, as we will explore in this chapter.

Defining Terms

Let's first pause to address several terms that will be helpful to define as we move into this chapter, namely *ethnicity, multiethnicity, diversity,* and *representation.*

Ethnicity, from the Greek word *ethnos*, is defined as "a social group that shares a common and distinctive culture, religion, language, or the like."[1] Korean, Italian, and Haitian are all examples of ethnicities. In the Bible, you will often find the Greek word *ethnos* translated as "nation" or "people," such as in Acts 2:5: "There were staying in Jerusalem God-fearing Jews from every nation [*ethnos*] under heaven."

Multiethnicity refers to a collection of more than one ethnic group in contrast to *monoethnicity*, which means only one ethnic group. God is the creator of all the ethnic groups in this world, and when we reach the end of time, individuals—from all these groups—who have embraced a saving knowledge of Jesus will celebrate him.

Another term you may hear frequently in conversations about race is **diversity**. When we talk about diversity, we mean the full range of all of God's creation, everything listed in Genesis 1, including stars and planets, birds and animals, vegetation and humans. By itself, diversity isn't a negative or positive idea. For our purposes here, it just means that a particular group or context reflects a range of different kinds of people from a variety of ethnic backgrounds.

Representation refers to the idea that the multiethnic range of people whom God has created should be reflected throughout relevant social systems and structures. The goal of representation isn't for every space to be representative of every distinct ethnic and cultural group that exists; that wouldn't be practical or even feasible. In South Korea, for example, it's not realistic to expect that people from, say, China or Italy or Nigeria should be represented in the country's leadership. Rather, the goal of representation is for any given space to reflect the people in its community and/or country. In this book, we are focusing on North America, where there is no justification for why significant imbalances exist, especially given our increasingly diverse demographics. For example, if you look at the CEOs of *Fortune* 500 companies, you'll find that 86 percent of them are white men even though that group represents only 35 percent of the

American population.[2] So, in the US, *representation* refers to the intentional inclusion of underrepresented voices. We will be focusing on ethnic and cultural representation in our discussion, although the term can be used in other contexts with regard to other categories.

A God Who Values Multiethnicity

One of my (Helen's) favorite hobbies is bird-watching. The Bible does, after all, say, "Consider the birds" (Matthew 6:26, CSB)! On a beautiful day, I can spend hours of Sabbath time sitting outside and watching all manner of feathered friends enjoy the multiple forms of bird food I supply. (For now, let's put aside the fact that the Bible doesn't say, "Feed the birds," as my husband regularly teases me!) I absolutely marvel at the variety of flying creatures that frequent my yard, ranging from large hawks swooping overhead to miniscule hummingbirds whizzing by, their wings in constant motion. I often reflect on how much enjoyment God found in creating each one. I don't think it was a chore; I think it was an overflow of his creative spirit.

Unsurprisingly, God's creative spirit is manifest in the way he designed humanity. As the Bible says, "Are you not much more valuable than [the birds]?" (verse 26). There is a reason God created humankind with so much wondrous variety as opposed to making all of us the same. In our different ethnicities, appearances, languages, and more, God's value of diversity is on display. As Old Testament professor Bruce Waltke said of the creation account in Genesis 1–2, "All created species follow God's master design and appointed purposes."[3] Whether we are talking about the birds of the air, every kind of flower and tree, or people, the opening chapters of the Bible declare that God delights in a universe that reflects his incredible creativity, especially as "all his works everywhere in his dominion" praise him in full submission and worship (Psalm 103:22).

In Scripture, God also repeatedly demonstrates his love for

humankind as a multiethnic body. From the creation mandate for humans to "be fruitful and multiply" (Genesis 1:28; 9:7, NLT) to the diversification of people into numerous tribes and languages at the tower of Babel (Genesis 11:1–9), we see God's commitment to humans flourishing as a multiethnic group. Creating human beings who reflect multiethnic diversity was God's idea from the very beginning, and it is also part of what it means to be made in God's own image—the Godhead itself is three diverse, unique persons in one. Moreover, from God's promise to Abraham, which included a name change such that he became "the father of many nations" (Genesis 17:5), to God's willingness to save the Assyrian capital of Nineveh in the book of Jonah, to the multiple ways that Jesus showed love to people groups whom the Jews thought of as outside God's mercy and grace (i.e., Samaritans and Gentiles of various ethnic backgrounds), God showed that he embraces people from every nation (Acts 10:34–35) even when human beings don't do the same for one another.

God has clearly valued multiethnicity from the earliest days of the church, which was given the directive to share the gospel "in Jerusalem, and in all Judea and Samaria, and to the ends of the earth" (Acts 1:8). In Acts 2, the apostles, full of the Holy Spirit, began speaking in languages they didn't know: "God-fearing Jews from every nation under heaven ... heard their own languages being spoken" (verses 5–6). In this moment, a multicultural group of Jews broke out in a multilingual choir of sound. The beauty of this significant day is not that people's ethnicities were erased but that their differences were bridged. God did not brush over the ethnic differences of the people in Jerusalem, but he leaned into those differences and used them to bring more people to a saving knowledge of himself. More than three thousand people became Christians that day. Clearly, the gospel goes forth *when* we celebrate diverse peoples, languages, and cultures. Pentecost offers a truth we so often fail to embody: God's dream is for his followers to reflect his love for diversity, not homogeneity.

The principle of multiethnicity applies just as much today as it did at Pentecost. My (Helen's) friend James Choung is a second-generation Korean American. His wife, Jinhee, is formerly a Korean national who immigrated to the US after they got married. James notes that when he says, "I love you," Jinhee understands what he is saying. But when he says, "*Saranghae,*" that touches her in an indescribably deep way because Korean is her heart language. Ethnic identity and experience are key channels through which God delivers the gospel and calls people—in their heart languages—to their heavenly home. Jesus himself reached across gender, class, generational, religious, and ethnic lines in order to declare his lordship over all and to proclaim his gospel message to everyone. Jesus valued ethnicity and culture, and we as individuals and as families are called to do the same.

Finally, God repeatedly foreshadowed in his Word what will ultimately happen when every tongue, tribe, and nation worships before the throne (Revelation 7:9–10). For example, in Daniel 7 we read,

> In my vision at night I looked, and there before me was one like a son of man, coming with the clouds of heaven. He approached the Ancient of Days and was led into his presence. He was given authority, glory and sovereign power; all nations and peoples of every language worshiped him. His dominion is an everlasting dominion that will not pass away, and his kingdom is one that will never be destroyed. (verses 13–14)

Daniel 7 and Revelation 7 remind us that "multiethnicity is that dream, that ideal [realized], that all of God's people—of every tribe, tongue, and nation—are welcome and cherished in God's kingdom. It is the hope and vision of a community of Christ followers that represent the diversity of God's creation."[4] We will exist as a diverse people group for all eternity. Moreover, the purpose of teaching our children to value people of every language is not to have multiethnicity for multiethnicity's sake but to show-case the power of unifying in worship before the Lord Almighty. The barriers that often exist when people of every stripe and color are together vanish as they collectively focus their full attention on God.

> **The barriers that often exist when people of every stripe and color are together vanish as they collectively focus their full attention on God.**

Our primary identity as Christians is that we are citizens of God's kingdom and coheirs with the rest of God's chosen people. Our spiritual identity, however, doesn't diminish our ethnic identities. God values the diverse ethnic groups he created, and we will retain our ethnic and cultural identities in the new heaven and the new earth. Similarly, God is calling us, as race-wise families, to acknowledge and respect the diverse ethnic contexts of the people in our lives.

Why We Need Multiethnic Understanding

According to recent population projections, the United States will become a non-white nation by 2045.[5] Lest we think this is still a faraway reality, for our kids who are fifteen years old and younger, the nation's future demographic reality is *already* the case. Fifty percent of this age group is non-white.[6] For this reason and more, it is imperative for race-wise parents to be actively communicating God's posture of valuing multiethnicity and embracing it ourselves in our families.

Sadly, we can't rely on the body of Christ to do this automatically. In the North American church, there is evidence of postures and preferences that aren't in alignment with God's example and intent. According to a 2018 survey by the Public Religion Research Institute, "a majority (54%) of white evangelical Protestants say that becoming [a] majority-nonwhite nation in the future will be mostly negative."[7] When the family of God prefers that its composition remain largely monoethnic, fissures and a reduced witness are inevitable.

Jemar Tisby, author of the *New York Times* bestselling book *The Color of Compromise,* is quoted in the *Washington Post* as saying, "As long as white evangelicals either consciously or subconsciously assume that American means white or European descended, they will always perceive changing demographics as a threat to 'the American way.' "[8] The body of Christ still has a long way to go before we collectively value multiethnicity in the way our heavenly Father does.

It is equally dangerous to assume that the presence of different cultures alone is sufficient to ensure that the needs and concerns of people of color are being seen and heard. Sometimes well-meaning Christians think that as long as people of color are present somewhere in the system, then all shall be well. But there is a difference between representation and creating a truly multiethnic community and culture.

In January 2021, a well-known megachurch posted a video intended to teach children about the Bible. It featured a white pastor dressed in a Chinese shirt, making stereotypical martial arts sounds and then spitting out sushi he had made. The church received a flood of complaints, the video was removed, and both the lead pastor and the church issued apologies for the cultural misstep. While the content might have been thought to represent Asian culture, it actually did much more harm than good. In his apology, the pastor indicated that the video demonstrated cultural and racial insensitivity, and it was an inappropriate way to teach children and their parents.

How did such a misguided teaching tool even get created in the first place? Perhaps Asian Americans weren't consulted at all, or if they were, those who were asked for feedback either didn't feel comfortable being honest about their concerns or may not have been culturally sensitive enough to be aware of how the content could be damaging.

Pursuing multiethnicity isn't just about getting one or two people to vet ideas that could ultimately prove to be offensive or insensitive. Instead, it is about making the systemic or structural changes needed to ensure that the experiences and voices of people of color will be fairly and

> **Pursuing multiethnicity means we must enjoy one another in all our diverse personalities, idiosyncrasies, and ethnic backgrounds with the aim of uplifting one another.**

appropriately represented and heard. It is about understanding how power plays a role in these discussions and dynamics and then finding ways to empower those who are on the margins.

Representation is important, and diversity is also needed in the books we read and the shows we watch as well as in the churches, organizations, communities, and schools we are part of. However, diversity and representation aren't enough. We must give honor and deference to each person's culture as well. Thus, pursuing multiethnicity means we must enjoy one another in all our diverse personalities, idiosyncrasies, and ethnic backgrounds with the aim of appreciating and edifying one another—not treating someone else's culture as a prop or the brunt of a joke. As we lean into valuing one another, we will experience the power of our witness as the multiethnic body of Christ.

Unfortunately, our ethnic uniqueness hasn't always been valued. Instead, we have both often experienced the sting of exclusion and occasions when it was clear that our presence was problematic precisely because of our ethnicities. I (Helen) can keenly recall the way I felt throughout the COVID-19 pandemic, especially when it was being repeatedly termed "the Kung Flu" and "the Chinese virus." Whenever I was out grocery shopping for the family, I felt fearful and nervous with every sideways glance in my direction. When people of color and those of mixed identity—in other words, those who are non-white—experience being stigmatized or being seen as "the other," they feel the opposite of valued; they can experience trauma and feel shame about their God-given ethnicity. This isn't how God intends any of us to feel about how he created us.

Here in the US, because of our increasingly multiethnic demographics, we have an opportunity to provide a beautiful foretaste of Revelation 7 in a way that many other nations do not. Pursuing multiethnicity today means making space for different peoples and cultures in ways that honor them. It's a posture that will require us to learn about ourselves and others and to love one another and work together despite our differences. Whether or not multiethnicity is being addressed in our churches, we parents need to teach our kids about topics like these: Why did God choose to create humankind in different shades and ethnicities? What purpose do these differences serve in addition to giving God pleasure? How do we show people of other ethnicities and cultures that we value them as fellow human beings?

We believe that God's intent is for all of us to lean into the beautiful differences inherent in the body of Christ and to demonstrate in no uncertain terms that the love of Christ ultimately overcomes all barriers and binds his people—his diverse and multiethnic people—in such perfect unity that "the world will know that [God] sent [him]" (John 17:23).

Practices to Value Multiethnicity as a Race-Wise Family

As race-wise parents, we must teach our children to value multiethnicity so that we can honor, celebrate, and utilize the diversity God has given us for the sake of his kingdom. The following are suggested practices that you and your kids can adopt to develop a posture of valuing multiethnicity, and doing so will bring you closer to the heart of God. Embracing these practices will also help bring healing and unity to the body of Christ as people from a variety of ethnic and cultural backgrounds begin to experience being seen and valued by other Christians. The church could become an incredible example of Christian witness and unity if we begin to be more like Christ in our love for people who are unlike us, especially non-white, often-marginalized groups who still experience the trauma of rejection from their fellow citizens here in the US. It just takes a posture of valuing our multiethnic body, binding ourselves together in our Savior's perfect love.

1. Discuss God's creative design and love for diversity with your children while going on a color walk. You might think of it like a treasure hunt where the treasure is color. Choose any colors you like, let your children choose their favorite colors, or look for all the colors of the rainbow. Then walk through your house (if you have young children) or go on a walk outside together. You can photograph or draw each thing you find, write down what you see, or just look around. In addition, you can go to the zoo, a museum, or an arboretum/botanical garden and make a list of all the new and/or unique things you see, including their colors.

2. Read stories and books by diverse authors who honor different cultural and ethnic backgrounds by depicting their characters in positive, redeeming ways (see appendix 3 for a list of recommended titles). Children of all ages can benefit from being surrounded by these kinds of books, which are growing in number each day. As you learn about people different from yourselves, continue to point to God's posture of valuing multiethnicity in order to impress on your children that this is God's heart and intention.

3. As a family, investigate the ethnic heritage of your neighborhood, city, or region. Visit or call the local chamber of commerce or historical society to find out more about the indigenous populations who first lived in your area and

about the immigration patterns that emerged over time. Find out what, if any, ethnic celebrations happen in your area, and make a point to attend these together on a regular basis.

4. Take virtual trips to other countries. Check out services such as Dorina Lazo Gilmore-Young's monthly membership *Global Glory Chasers: Traveling the World from the Comfort of Your Home,* in which she and her family curate these travel experiences with a variety of recipes, books, movies, and music to easily bring cultures from around the world into your own home. On her website, Dorina wrote, "We believe God uniquely created each one of us in His image. If we want to grow in our understanding of God, we need to grow in our knowledge about each other."[9] We couldn't agree more.

5. Learn about cultural occasions and holidays from around the world. What is Lunar New Year, for example? Who celebrates it and how? You can do the same with Diwali, Día de los Muertos (Day of the Dead), Hanukkah, Kwanzaa, or any number of other ethnic holidays. These occasions are opportunities to teach your children about the blessing of the multiethnic world God has created and to make sure they know that the biggest celebration at the end of time will be like all these other special events combined—times a million—as we worship God together.

6. Regularly pray for people groups around the world. A wonderful resource to use for regular family devotional times is the book *Window on the World,* written by the leaders of Operation World. A comprehensive guide to understanding and praying for various people groups around the world, *Window on the World* is written with young children in mind, although the content can be just as helpful for teens and adults. Each chapter provides educational information about a particular country or people group and its culture as well as facts about its reli-

gious demographics and suggestions for praying for that people group.

7. Offer the following prayer either in your own devotional time or with your family:

Creator God,
You intentionally formed distinct cultures and ethnicities
as a reflection of your diverse design for creation and as a way to
draw all nations closer to yourself. We thank you that you
demonstrate your love for humankind in and through a
multiethnic body. Instill in our family a true love for
multiethnicity, not for diversity's sake alone but rather out of a
deep conviction that you showcase the power of unity when all of
us together worship before you, the Lord Almighty. May we
intentionally cultivate space for multiethnicity in our home,
our church, and our community in order to bring healing and
unity to the body of Christ, and may people from a variety
of ethnic and cultural backgrounds begin to sense that
they are seen and valued by other Christians. We recognize that it
is only through this means that the church will become an
incredible example of Christian witness and unity.
God, may we be your hands and feet.
Amen.

Seeing Color

HAVE YOU EVER WISHED you could change the way people see you? For the entirety of my childhood, my (Helen's) deep desire was to not be seen as a Korean American. I had been ostracized and bullied enough times as a kid for being the only person of Asian descent, not to mention one of the very few people of color, in my school. As I grew into adolescence, all I wanted was for other people to view me with color-blinders on so that my Korean ethnicity would fade into the background and I could be "just Helen." While everyone else in my family ate with chopsticks, I always chose to use a fork. Even with my closest friends, I tried to present an exterior that was assimilated to the majority culture, although before long some random stranger would burst my identity bubble with a comment such as "Your English is so good!"

"Well, that is because I am a natural-born American!" I would retort. But I would never say, "Korean American."

It wasn't until I was in college that God revealed a life-changing message to me through a group of Asian American mentors and friends: my ethnic identity was not a curse but a blessing. God designed me to be Korean for a beautiful purpose.

For all my childhood, I had tried to run away from my ethnicity. Now I was starting to understand that being fully seen meant I needed to embrace my Korean heritage and not hide it. These friends helped me recognize a key quality about how God created humankind: He had a deliberate eye toward the beauty of our distinct ethnic roots and cultural identities. Why had no one ever shared this fundamental truth with me before—and especially no one in the church?

When we became parents, my Korean Canadian husband, Brian, and I made intentional choices to help communicate to our three boys that their ethnic identity was something to be seen and celebrated. We gave all three of them Korean middle names and exposed them to the Korean language during their first year. Also, to the delight of all their grandparents, eating Korean food—including fistfuls of the traditional Korean side dish of kimchi (pickled, fermented cabbage)—was a given as soon as they transitioned to finger foods. Most importantly, all three of our boys have heard from birth that God has given them a wonderful gift in their Korean ethnicity, whether or not other people recognize and celebrate that gift.

Even in our increasingly multiethnic society, those who are from the majority culture—in the US, this generally means those who are white—often assume that people of color want to just be absorbed into that culture. When it comes to conversations with fellow Christians, Michelle and I both have heard statements such as "I don't see color; I just see you" or "Our cultural identities don't matter. Let's just be brothers and sisters in Christ. We're supposed to be one united body, right?"

The posture of *seeing color*, however, is a hallmark of a race-wise family. This posture reflects our understanding that we follow a God who has created people with distinct ethnic and cultural identities. Our kids should know the wonderful, unique ways that God has created them as human beings, from their skin and hair color to their ethnic roots. More than that, they should delight in and celebrate their God-given ethnic roots. Who they are culturally should be a point of pride, not shame.

> **Ethnic blindness can lead to misunderstandings and tensions at best and hatred, violence, and genocide at worst.**

If we can't see and celebrate the colors and cultures of the people God has created, then how can we adequately address issues related to race in our families and communities? Blindness of any kind keeps us from properly seeing God, ourselves, other people, and the world around us. Ethnic blindness can lead to misunderstandings and tensions at best and hatred, violence, and genocide at worst.

We were created to live in the fullness of our identity in Christ, and this includes who we are as cultural image bearers. The more we celebrate our cultural identities, the more we will be able to rejoice in the identities of others. In fact, the more we recognize and honor ethnic differences, including our own God-given heritages, the more we will be able to truly love the people around us and build the foundation for racial harmony within the body of Christ and beyond.

Defining Terms

In conversations today, *ethnicity* and *culture* are often interchanged and used inconsistently in our broader society. It can be confusing at times to know which term to use. Let's take a deeper dive into how these words relate to other important terms such as *multiculturalism* and *race*.

Culture is a person's whole way of life. The term has become a way to describe "the arts, beliefs, customs, institutions, and other products of human work and thought considered as a unit, especially with regard to a particular time or social group."[1] We define *culture* as being broader than just products and artifacts; it also includes stories and histories that align people with particular groups or generations. These narratives of culture become evident in our view of the world and our place in it as well as in how we communicate and relate with one another. Although the word doesn't appear in the Bible, it's used by Eugene Peterson in *The Message*. In his version of Romans 12:2, he wrote, "Don't become so well-adjusted to your culture that you fit into it without even thinking. Instead, fix your attention on God. You'll be changed from the inside out." So, one's culture is not just about tangible things that you can see, hear, and taste, but it's also about internal values and morals. As such, there is a subjective element to culture that is different from ethnicity, which has biological roots. For example, I (Helen) am ethnically Korean but culturally Korean American, while I (Michelle) am a bicultural Indian American raised with a mixture of Indian and white American cultural values.

Multicultural means the equal presence and value of more than one distinct cultural group, which can include but go beyond ethnic groups. It's a word that you might hear in conjunction with the idea of inclusion, especially when an organization is attempting to affirm the full range of cultural perspectives that exist in its structure (for example, a corporation recruiting diverse leadership or a church offering bilingual or multilingual church services). But as Christians, we know that not all cultural values and expressions honor God; here in the US, we can think of numerous cultural values and expressions that are idolatrous or otherwise problematic (such as materialism, machismo, or hedonism, to name a few). Although we appreciate the ways in which multiculturalism seeks to value ethnic groups, at the same time we Christians must continually consider which aspects of our various cultures reflect the image of God and which aspects don't and therefore need to be addressed. Pursuing multiculturalism has to be accompanied by discernment so that what we advocate for in the name of multiculturalism is in line with God's desires for his people.

We'll discuss **race** more fully in posture 3; but for now, a quick summary is that it's generally a term that describes certain per-

> **We Christians must continually consider which aspects of our various cultures reflect the image of God and which aspects don't and therefore need to be addressed.**

ceived physical characteristics such as skin color, and those distinctions are then used to create hierarchies of value. In addition to *White*, official US racial categories include terms such as *Black/African American, American Indian, Asian,* and *Native Hawaiian/Other Pacific Islander* (Hispanic or Latino/a is considered an ethnic category).[2] We are both grouped into the racial category of Asian. Ethnically, however, I (Helen) am second-generation Korean American, while I (Michelle) am second-generation Indian American. My mother is 100 percent ethnically Indian, born in Uganda, Africa, as a result of the Indian diaspora. My father has British and German roots and can trace his relatives back to the Daughters of the American Revolution. *Second-generation* refers to the fact that our parents were the first generation in our families to immigrate to the US. Culturally speaking, we can each name multiple influences based on our unique heritage and experiences that define us. I (Helen) am a product of the East Coast, now live in the Midwest, am firmly in midlife, and have Korean Canadian American children. I (Michelle) grew up in the Midwest, now live in the South, and have Indian Mexican American kids. All these factors influence each of us culturally. The two of us are uniquely designed just as you are, and we each reflect in our heritage and experiences the inventive work of our creative God.

The Biblical Benefits of Seeing Color

When cultural and ethnic distinctives are seen and not ignored, amazing things can happen in the church and the world, as por-

trayed in Acts 6. Here a conflict was brewing between two seg-
ments of the early church: the Hellenistic (or Greek-cultured)
Jews and the Hebraic Jews. As Jews, these two groups shared the
same ethnic lineage, but one group had taken on the language
and customs of the majority culture (Hellenistic Jews), and the
other had retained their language and customs (Hebraic Jews).

The story in Acts 6 reminds me (Helen) of when I visited
Seoul, South Korea, for the first time. I felt out of place: it didn't
matter that I shared ethnicity with all the inhabitants around
me. My American-accented Korean was a clear sign that I
wasn't from Seoul, not to mention the way I dressed, among
other clues that would have been evident to a native resident. I
didn't always feel welcome or included by the native Koreans I
encountered who would make comments about my less-than-
perfect Korean or critique my American-style clothes.

Perhaps the Hellenistic Jews felt similarly slighted by their
ethnic kinfolk. We see in verse 1 that they had complained. As
one scholar noted, "It is not hard to imagine what the tensions
may have been, if the two parties are defined over-against each
other in linguistic and therefore in cultural terms."[3] Instead of
speaking Hebrew and maintaining fully Jewish customs, the
Hellenistic Jews spoke Greek and took on other cultural influences that reflected the Greek culture of their time. It's also
likely that these Hellenistic Jews had been part of the Diaspora;
that is, they had grown up and lived in cities outside of Jerusalem and then returned for different reasons.[4] In other words, the
Hellenistic Jews were immigrants, perceived foreigners, trying
to settle in a new land and city and not fully feeling like they fit
in socially or even religiously. As New Testament scholar James
Dunn explained, the cultural differences between the Hebraic
and Hellenistic Jews almost certainly resulted in "a degree of
suspicion and possibly even hostility between the two groups."[5]

The cultural conflict between Hebraic and Hellenistic Jews
caused injustice to arise. The Hellenistic widows weren't receiving their proper amount of the daily distribution of food in
this community that had developed a system for sharing re-

sources equitably. In her book *Beyond Colorblind*, Sarah Shin noted that the solution was to hire seven men, who became the first deaconate in the church and who—based on the etymology of their names—all appear to have been Hellenistic.[6] The church's solution was to right the previous wrongs by ensuring *more* than adequate representation of Hellenistic believers in this new group of leaders. God didn't create a fifty-fifty split between Hebraic and Hellenistic Jewish leaders. Instead, his solution had a strong ethnic component and ensured equity, demonstrating that he had heard the voices of the Hellenistic Christians who had raised the concerns.

More than that, God ensured the recognition and empowerment of a culturally defined minority group. In the case of the early church and the conflict between the Hebraic and Hellenistic Jews, the solution was to *see* the ethnic group that had been slighted or ignored, address any injustices, and demonstrate that, though culturally different, the two groups were valued equally in God's eyes. Neither group was wrong or right; the two groups were equal in value but just different. The result of this reconciliation was that "the word of God spread [and] the number of disciples in Jerusalem increased rapidly" (Acts 6:7), quite a cause for celebration. In this cornerstone city of the Jewish people, seeing the just treatment of both Hellenistic and Hebraic Jews drew people from all over the city to faith in Jesus. In the same way, when we fully see people, we can truly care for them. Seeing color affirms each person's ethnic identity and heritage as well as finds ways to ensure that people of color or other marginalized voices are heard and heeded. The example in Acts 6 sets a precedent for how we are to see and celebrate all cultures, especially those on the margins.

Becoming Color Aware

If God sees and values the colors of those he has created, why do so many people remain committed to being color-blind?

Color blindness dismisses distinctions between people groups. This posture often arises out of good intentions. For example, sometimes parents attempt to minimize differences by saying, "I don't see color" or "We as a family don't see color." The statement "I don't see color" is also a backlash against the overt racism that was prominent during the civil rights movement. However, the posture of color blindness causes more harm than good. Early-childhood educator Madeleine Rogin said,

> When we shush a child for noticing a racial difference, or when they say something misguided or biased, they don't stop noticing or forming biases, they just learn to keep these observations and ideas to themselves.[7]

Many of us people of color, including children,[8] *want* to be seen in all the beauty and diversity of our ethnic backgrounds. We don't want our distinctiveness melted away into the majority (typically white) culture. To be told otherwise actually creates more division than unity.

The choice by many families to be color-blind has led to damaging effects especially for blended families and those who have transracially adopted children. We both have friends who are transracial adoptees, adopted at birth by Christian parents who chose to never teach them about their home country or culture in an attempt to be a color-blind family. Some of these adoptees were even taught to reject their ethnic roots in order to embrace—and be accepted by—their new family. These now-grown men and women have suffered deep pain and loss as a result.

In her book *Beyond Colorblind*, Shin wrote,

> Colorblindness, though well intentioned, is inhospitable. . . .
> We need something beyond colorblindness, something that both values beauty in our cultures and also addresses real problems that still exist in our society decades after the civil rights movement.[9]

Think about that quote for a moment. To not see color as a family is to choose to be inhospitable to people around us. By choosing a posture of color blindness, how many Christian families have unknowingly done the opposite of loving their neighbors?

There is no doubt in our minds that the race-related problems that still plague our country are partially due to the fact that so many Christians and Christian families affirm the teaching that we are "one human race," which denies both the beauty of God's diverse creation and the challenges that exist in our nation because of racial and ethnic differences. When we and our children embrace a color-blind mentality, we are living in opposition to the gospel mandate to be reconcilers— reconciled first to God and then to one another (2 Corinthians 5:18). Color blindness is a barrier to that process of reconciliation.

Rather than being color-blind, we parents must teach our children how to be culturally aware, to be "color aware"—and doing so requires intentionality on our part. Too often our children are programmed by society and the church alike to not think about the color of their skin or whether they are part of the dominant or a subdominant culture. As a young girl, I (Michelle) even thought that I was white because the recurring lesson I heard was that "we are all the same." But we're not the same, even those of us who are racially white. A positive first step that we can take as race-wise parents is to give our children time and space to take a long, deep look at their skin colors, hair colors, and bodies; what their ancestry and ethnic roots mean to them; and how their stories, experiences, and cultural values affect the way they live.

Seeing color in Scripture will also empower race-wise families to see color within their own homes. When you read Scripture, do you default to imagining people in the Bible as white? For many years, the painting by Warner Sallman called *The Head of Christ,* which depicts Jesus with an incandescent glow about his face and distinctly European features, was the standard portrait that many American Christians possessed, and it shaped their ideas of what Jesus looked like. Even my (Helen's) Korean American family owned a small reproduction of this painting, and it was how I grew up imagining Jesus. No one ever told me as a child that Jesus wouldn't actually look that way as a Middle Eastern man! Nor would most of the other key figures in Scripture.

As we all take steps to become more ethnically and culturally aware, we begin to see our own cultural distinctiveness as well as that of others. And our children will come to see how unsatisfying it is to paint ourselves and others into one monolithic, colorless blob—and how much more meaningful and in fact biblical it is to discover all the colorful shades of humanity.

Practices to See Color as a Race-Wise Family

Help your kids stand against color blindness and instead see color with eyes of truth and hope. Research shows that even babies can identify racial differences, so the reality is that they are *already* seeing distinctions between people.[10] But if those uniquenesses are never discussed in the home, then kids (and adults) will develop their own interpretations of those differences, and not all of those will be in line with God's wisdom and vision for human beings.

Here are some activities you can do as a family to develop the right kind of vision and become race-wise in the way you view those around you:

1. An important first step as parents seeking to help your family become biblically race-wise is to see color in Scripture. Buy your children a Bible in which people are depicted with the brown skin of the Middle East (see appendix 3 for suggestions). Spend time identifying different Bible characters' ethnic identities, naming them aloud with your children, finding on a map where they

lived, and even discussing what they might have looked like.

2. Spend time exploring your family's ethnic roots. Each one of us has a unique story, though here in the United States, tracing your lineage and discovering cultural influences might take a little more time and effort. If you are from a non-Native context, when did your family arrive in the US? If your family is Native, what tribe(s) are a part of your story? What stories can you recall or discover about your ancestors that demonstrate an ethnic allegiance, connection, or custom? Taking a DNA test can add another piece to your ethnic identity puzzle and may be worth pursuing.

3. Get in touch with elements of your family's story that you are unfamiliar with. Perhaps you have a relative from several generations back who came from a country you don't know much about. Ask yourself how you can get to know more about that relative or what conversations you can have with living relatives who can help you with any gaps in your understanding. Consider using a service such as StoryWorth to gather these stories in a way that can be preserved in perpetuity.

4. Think of ways your family can delight in and celebrate your unique cultural identities. For example, you could spend time identifying and complimenting the similarities and differences in your skin colors and physical features. It's common in mixed families for parents and children to all have different skin tones, and these differences can become the springboard for conversations about God's beautiful design in making people different. Whether or not you all share the same skin color, thank God for how he created your family and for how he created people of other skin colors as well. You can also start the regular practice of sharing with your kids favorite stories and memories related to your heritage so that they, too, can better appreciate their ethnicity. Lean into

traditions, specific foods, clothing, and other cultural expressions from your family's heritage to celebrate who you are as cultural beings. The more you celebrate the distinctive ethnic and cultural markers of your family, the more you can reaffirm with your kids that their ethnic makeup is part of God's great story and vision for diversity.

5. When you meet with other families, make it a habit to ask what kinds of customs and traditions they follow and whether there are any cultural influences present. You will often find that customs and traditions with strong cultural ties have been passed down through the generations, and asking about them can be a way to honor those influences.

6. Begin to use racial and ethnic identifiers verbally as a family. Don't shy away from them. There is nothing wrong with stating the fact that people are created as unique beings with cultural distinctiveness. The more comfortable you are talking about racial and ethnic differences, the more your children will learn that there is nothing wrong with seeing and naming characteristics of race.

7. If you are in the majority culture, it can be harder to see color because you may be used to being surrounded by people who look like you. Seek opportunities to visit a cultural context where you are in the minority, such as a Black church, an Asian grocery store, or a Latino community. Spend time in that context as a family. Then afterward talk about it: What was it like to be in a space like that? How did you feel being in the minority? What did that experience help you understand about the experiences of people of color in white-dominant settings?

8. Ask your kids about the racial and ethnic makeup of the various spaces they inhabit, such as their schools, extracurricular activities, church groups, and so on. In any of those places, are there one or very few kids of color? If so,

ask whether there is any marginalization happening and discuss how your kids could be bridge builders. If you live in a more multiethnic setting, talk about group dynamics and whether there are any tensions between particular groups of kids. To more easily see color in everyday life, make it a habit to bring observations related to race and racial dynamics into your home.

9. At your workplace and elsewhere, become more aware of marginalized people whom you have never noticed. Do you work in a white-dominant setting? Are you attuned to whether colleagues of color are isolated and marginalized? As you take steps to increase your own awareness of ethnicity, you will also become aware of the cultural dynamics that are present for people of color. And you may find ways that you need to advocate for or learn from those colleagues.

10. Offer the following prayer either in your own devotional time or with your family:

God of Color and Beauty,
Guide our family to become more ethnically and culturally aware.
May we see what you see so that we can become attuned to our
own cultural distinctiveness and the cultural distinctiveness of
others. May our children believe and see that you created a colorful
world on purpose. May we discover how unsatisfying it is to paint
ourselves and others into a monolithic, colorless form. Help us live
into our embodied experiences as cultural beings so we can
appreciate and give thanks for all the colorful shades of humanity
that you created.
Amen.

Understanding a Biblical View of Racism

No MATTER HOW many decades have passed, I (Helen) can still remember with perfect clarity the first time I experienced the sting of a racial slur. I was in junior high school, just trying to get from geography to Spanish class, when a fellow seventh grader brushed by me. I had never even spoken to him, but right before he passed me, he muttered a slur under his breath yet loudly enough for me to hear. I caught the disdain in his direct gaze as I walked by. I can recall the combination of embarrassment and shame I felt in that moment, an experience that was repeated in different settings in the years to come when others tossed my way the same slur or variations of it. Although as a preteen I didn't have the language to articulate it, I knew instinctively that what I had experienced was an instance of racism.

Fast-forward to the present day when my eldest son and I were discussing the racial incident that I shared in the introduction of this book, the time when he had been victimized verbally and on social media. Now seventeen years old, he was inclined to downplay the incident and call it an instance of immaturity or just teasing from the other boys.

"No," I gently corrected him. "It wasn't just teasing. It was a racial taunt, using racialized language, and we have to call those instances what they are."

But my son isn't the only one I know who has been unsure about how to name certain behaviors and attitudes that cross the line into racism. Even in the church today, there is a great deal of confusion about this topic and disagreement over what should be categorized as racism. Some Christians believe that there is too much emphasis on the topic of race and that this overemphasis has become a divisive idol in the church today. Others might feel the exact opposite—that there isn't nearly enough conversation about race and that the church lets too much slide when racism should be confronted and eradicated. Who is right?

We believe that a healthy perspective on the topic of race avoids both extremes. There can be danger on both ends of the spectrum, whether emphasizing issues of race to a fault or not emphasizing them enough. Given that the church lacks agreement in this area, which also damages our Christian witness to the world, perhaps we could all benefit from seeking common ground—rather than acting like our kids sometimes do when two or more are in a conflict and no one wants to budge.

Racism is a modern term. It wouldn't have been part of the language of the ancient Near East or the first-century world. Nevertheless, while the word *racism* doesn't appear in the Bible, the reality of racism is still abundantly clear. Moreover, many biblical principles speak to how we are to conduct ourselves as individuals and as the church when it comes to the issue of race. In fact, the Bible gives us all the principles we need to help us understand racism, explain it to our children, and chart a way to live in a society that will continue to struggle with this issue until Jesus returns.

Defining Terms

Before we turn to those principles, we want to define the terms we will use in this chapter. First, **race** generally refers to the categorization of people based on common physical features, in particular, skin color. The first official categorization of race in the United States occurred with the first census in 1790. At that time, people were assigned to one of three categories: slaves, free white females and males, and all other free persons.[1] Since then, these categories have continued to shift, partly to provide a foundation for restrictive immigration laws that, until the 1960s, largely favored people of European ancestry. Undoubtedly, these shifts will continue as the demographics of the US change, but understanding race goes beyond merely acknowledging categories.

We choose to define *race* not only as the categorization of people groups based on physical characteristics such as skin color but also as a system designed to give advantages to certain groups, especially those who are white in the United States. Race includes the power structures that assign value to these categories of people since not all groups are valued equally in our country.

What are those categories? According to recent US census data, race is articulated in our country in the following ways:

- white
- Black or African American
- American Indian or Alaska Native
- Asian
- Native Hawaiian or other Pacific Islander
- some other race
- two or more races[2]

The increasing number of people who identify with one or more racial categories in the United States tells you that racial preferences, barriers, and traumas still exist. Race isn't just what a census form tags you. It includes the ways in which the systems and structures of our country demonstrate favoritism toward one racial group—which, in the United States, means those who are white—over all others.

According to sociologist David Wellman in his 1977 book, *Portraits of White Racism,* **racism** is a system of advantage based on race.[3] In other words, racism is a combination of prejudice and power against people of color. It is a system that disadvantages anyone who is not white. It was just in June 2020 that *Merriam-Webster* decided to amend its definition of *racism* to include the dimension of power, thanks to the advocacy of a young Black woman who wrote to the editors and raised her concern about the limits of the existing definition. Even in a storied and well-known reference book, *racism* isn't always easy to define.

Then there is the question of what the Bible says about race. Numerous translations use the word *race* as a way to describe "the human race," which is not the way we are defining it here. In other words, translations that merely use the word *race* don't reflect the modern-day understanding of the word. For example, Romans 9:3–4 in the NIV reads, "I could wish that I myself were cursed and cut off from Christ for the sake of my people, those of my own race, the people of Israel." But in the original Greek, that word *race* is perhaps better translated as "kinsman." The Bible doesn't give us a term that is perfectly equivalent to the way the word *race* is used in our modern context, and as mentioned earlier, the word *racism* itself doesn't appear in the Bible at all. But then again, neither does *evangelism,* yet that doesn't prevent Christians from trying to understand how to be effective witnesses for the gospel. Similarly, we Christian parents need to keep trying to understand race and racism.

A Biblical Understanding of Race and Racism

God demonstrated his multiethnic vision from Genesis to Revelation, and people from all tribes, tongues, and nations will ultimately worship at his throne in an extraordinarily diverse display of unity. However, we have a long way to go to get from where we are to that Revelation 7 ideal. While it's beyond the scope of this book to dive into a full examination of where issues of race and racism began, here are a number of biblical points to keep in mind.

Racism Stems from the Overarching Effects of Sin (Individually and Corporately)

Racism didn't come out of a vacuum; it has an origin story of its own, going all the way back to the beginning of human history. Right on the heels of the Fall in Genesis 3, Cain killed Abel, and so began the long history of brothers turning against brothers. Since those early days of human history, we have seen the ways that sin has undergirded all manner of conflicts—including racial and ethnic tension—between people groups in our world. As we read in Paul's letter to the Romans,

> Jews and Gentiles alike are all under the power of sin. As it is written:
>
> > "There is no one righteous, not even one;
> > there is no one who understands;
> > there is no one who seeks God.
> > All have turned away,
> > they have together become worthless;
> > there is no one who does good,
> > not even one." (3:9–12)

Our disconnection from God results in our seeking every advantage and thinking of our own selves rather than choosing goodness and holiness.

On an individual level, racism is one way that we, in our sin nature, disregard the image of God that is present in each human being. None of us can claim to be unaffected by this sin nature. "You, therefore, have no excuse, you who pass judgment on someone else," Paul wrote in Romans 2, "for at whatever point you judge another, you are condemning yourself, because you who pass judgment do the same things" (verse 1). Sin mars the way we see both ourselves and other people. Sin also causes us to value certain people groups as better than others, and it is the source of the ugliness and hate that have been part of our broken world since the Fall.

The sin of racism is manifest in all levels of our society. We know this is true because all of creation has been distorted by sin (Romans 8:20–22). As US Catholic bishops noted forty years ago in their pastoral letter "Brothers and Sisters to Us,"

> the structures of our society are subtly racist, for these structures reflect the values which society upholds. They are geared to the success of the majority and the failure of the minority. Members of both groups give unwitting approval by accepting things as they are. Perhaps no single individual is to blame. The sinfulness is often anonymous but nonetheless real. The sin is social in nature in that each of us, in varying degrees, is responsible. All of us in some measure are accomplices.[4]

In other words, racism touches everyone's life. It is threaded through our history; it's in the air we breathe. It's not that racism didn't exist in centuries past and now it does, as some argue. Rather, with the rise of viral videos and social media, we are able to see more of the sin firsthand, such as the deaths of Michael Brown, George Floyd, Ahmaud Arbery, and Mike Ramos and the six Asian women murdered in the Atlanta shooting on March 16, 2021. As the pastoral letter also declares, "Racism is not merely one sin among many; it is a radical evil that divides the human family and denies the new creation of a redeemed world."[5]

Racism, then, is rooted in sin that causes people to rise up against other people to gain advantage in both individual and social relations. As the population on the earth grew, our sin nature resulted not just in individuals seeking to further themselves but also in people groups unifying around their cultural and nationalistic identities and then clashing with other people groups. We have seen the effects of these sinful patterns throughout history and into the current day. If you pick up the National Book Award–winning volume *Stamped from the Beginning: The Definitive History of Racist Ideas in America* by Ibram X. Kendi, for example, you will encounter nearly six hundred pages documenting the origins of racism here in the United States, starting back in the colonial days. Sadly, we know that nations will continue to rise against nations until God's kingdom is fully restored.

The Holistic Gospel Is the Solution to Racism

In the face of a racial tragedy, we too often hear that our sole response as Christians should be to preach the gospel. On the one hand, of course we as Christians are called to preach the gospel. But sometimes Christians have a limited understanding of what the gospel actually is. Some believe in a narrow view of the gospel that addresses only personal salvation, but the problem is that being saved is no guarantee that racism in a person's life will disappear. As we all know, throughout human history, Christians as well as non-Christians have perpetuated racism.

Undoubtedly, the road to ending hate involves repenting for our sin *and* living the gospel. We must understand from the life, ministry, and blood of Jesus Christ that the gospel is robust and active. As I (Michelle) argued in an article in the *Christianity Today* blog *The Better Samaritan:*

Jesus saves people holistically. We sees the ways that people suffer physically, socially, and spiritually and he offers himself as a balm to all of our pains and our brokenness. . . . This is why he calls for us to first repent and believe in his good news: repentance means turning away from sin, and faith means acknowledging dependence on God. These are two sides of the same coin: repudiating a life focused on self and reorienting toward God and his purpose for the world. But simultaneously Jesus is also healing people physically—those with physical disabilities, the blind, the lame, those with leprosy, the sick—so that they can be restored back into society. He cares about redeeming whole persons and [reintegrating] them into a restored community. The good news of the gospel is that Jesus seeks to make our world whole in every aspect of the term (as he says in Revelation 21:5 "I am making all things new").[6]

When we believe in and seek to embody the holistic gospel of Jesus, we are mindful of how we live and work in the world, how we care for our communities, how we care for our neighbors. If we are transformed by our relationship with Jesus, we should have a transformed view of both our neighbors and issues of life and justice. This means, on the one hand, that if we find ourselves thinking that Black people, Asians, Latinos, Native Americans, and/or immigrants are beneath us, we need to start here and ask God to address the sin in our hearts. It also means that as we seek to address the sin of racism, we should have the pursuit of restoration in mind. This restoration happens in both a vertical and a horizontal direction. We must seek to restore people not only to God (vertical) but also to each other and to our surrounding environment, both nature and social systems (horizontal). Addressing the sin of racism in our hearts *and* its manifestations in our society is one vital way we join Jesus in his gospel-centered work in the world.

Racism in the Church Taints Our Biblical Witness

Racism outside the body of Christ is to be expected because of our sin nature, but racism and ethnic conflict within the body are evidence that God's people aren't taking to heart the call to love one another the way God intends us to. In 1 John 4, the apostle wrote,

> We love because he first loved us. Whoever claims to love God yet hates a brother or sister is a liar. For whoever does not love their brother and sister, whom they have seen, cannot love God, whom they have not seen. And he has given us this command: Anyone who loves God must also love their brother and sister. (verses 19–21)

Anyone who loves God must also love their brother and sister. With racial division in the church today, we are losing an opportunity to witness in a world that desperately needs models of healthy cross-racial and cross-cultural relationships.

For Christians in the United States, standing against racism isn't merely avoiding bigotry and hatred of other racial groups. That is too low a bar. Our call is to a much higher standard: to proactively love those who are different from us and to examine the ways in which we knowingly or unknowingly support systems and structures that benefit any dominant group.

The ministry of reconciliation (2 Corinthians 5:18) is a call to show how the power of the whole gospel brings together people who might not naturally love one

> **Our call is to a much higher standard: to proactively love those who are different from us and to examine the ways in which we knowingly or unknowingly support systems and structures that benefit any dominant group.**

another. So as Christians, our calling is not only to respect the image of God in other people but *especially* to love those within the body of Christ who are different from us. This is what leads to true unity. Reducing, if not eradicating, racism is an intentional pursuit in which we seek to demonstrate love and respect across all differences. Dismantling racism is an extension of our call to love our neighbors, and it should be an active, daily living out of our faith. This love then becomes a witness to the world that leads others to follow Christ and embrace the same call to love their brothers and sisters in the church.

Seek Wisdom, Listen, and Learn

So, where do we start? Arguments and opinions from so many corners of the church can be confusing, whether we're talking about Black Lives Matter, critical race theory, or what constitutes appropriation, just to give a sampling of the many areas of disagreement. Thankfully, the Bible also gives us many models for how to determine whom to listen to. In 1 Corinthians 12, Paul wrote,

> God has placed the parts in the body, every one of them, just as he wanted them to be. If they were all one part, where would the body be? As it is, there are many parts, but one body.
>
> The eye cannot say to the hand, "I don't need you!" And the head cannot say to the feet, "I don't need you!" On the contrary, those parts of the body that seem to be weaker are indispensable, and the parts that we think are less honorable we treat with special honor. And the parts that are unpresentable are treated with special modesty, while our presentable parts need no special treatment. But God has put the body together, giving greater honor to the parts that lacked it, so that there should be no division in the body, but that its parts should have equal concern for each other. If one part suffers, every part suffers with it; if one part is honored, every part rejoices with it. (verses 18–26)

First Corinthians 12 is a model for how to pursue unity in the area of race in our churches. Whose voices have been muffled or silenced with regard to racial issues? Who is on the margins in the body of Christ? Whose opinions have been swept aside or ignored? Who needs to receive greater honor in order to prevent divisions within the body of Christ? For the majority of the history of the American church, those silenced voices have tended to belong to people of color. The pathway to unity—which allows the church to have an effective witness— is to give greater honor and credence to the voices on the margins, even if you don't agree with them.

For example, when a person of color tells you that he or she has experienced racism, is your gut reaction to say, "I believe you, and I'm sorry" or to dismiss the claim? We must challenge our hearts and our minds to believe those who are speaking out in pain. Their pain is real. As author Adrian Pei wrote, "The minority experience isn't primarily about head knowledge— but about emotional realities of pain."[7] Moreover, we must not only believe the stories of racism presented to us but also recognize that the realities of racism look different from one community to the next. As people of color, we need to listen to one another and give equal weight to the racism that we each experience in different ways. This doesn't mean that we immediately adopt every opinion of every Christian of color, but it does mean that we pay attention to those voices and listen for any common refrain or concept and that we humbly give those ideas a chance to permeate our own hearts, minds, and souls.

None of us are perfect in our understanding or convictions. We all have to be discerning in determining whose voices are Spirit led and truth filled. Ask God for wisdom, which he will generously give (James 1:5). If you are on a journey of learning, lean toward being "quick to listen [and] slow to speak" (verse 19) especially about matters of race. There is no downside to taking the time to listen and learn rather than being argumentative or vocal. As you find trustworthy voices from the margins to follow and learn from, as you gain insight into issues of race, and, most importantly, as you stay rooted in Scripture and pray for guidance to remain on the pathway of truth, God will deepen your understanding of both the causes of racism and biblical ways to root it out. Like all transformative processes, this takes time and patience. Give yourself grace as you continue onward, and trust that the Lord will keep revealing more about his intentions regarding racial issues.

Understanding the biblical view of racism is a lifelong journey, one that requires continual submission to the Spirit's leading. We know that at the end of time, in the Day of the Lord, people from every tongue, tribe, and nation will be gathered both to worship God and to be judged by him for all we have done and left undone. It is our firm belief that the US church will have to confront its sinful legacy of complicity with racial injustices both large and small and face how this legacy kept many from understanding and embracing the true gospel of Jesus Christ. The good news is that we still have time to experience transformation and to help our children do better than we parents have done in the pursuit of racial reconciliation and justice.

Practices to Understand Racism as a Race-Wise Family

1. Learn about US history from marginalized voices. Most of us grew up learning American history from sources that may not have presented the full story of our nation's founding. Whenever there is a key American holiday—Independence Day, Thanksgiving, or Indigenous Peoples' Day, for example—take the opportunity to present a different view of what is being celebrated. Use resources such as Families Embracing Diversity's website "Real US History for Kids"[8] to find helpful lists of resources and ideas for various age groups.

2. When it comes to explaining complex issues like race and racism to your kids, multimedia resources can be a help. Watch an age-appropriate movie, show, or video such as those suggested by the George Lucas Educational Foundation,[9] or see appendix 3 for other resources to consider. Ask your kids the following questions, as appropriate for their ages:

    a. How did watching this show make you feel? What was the most powerful thing you saw? What had the most impact on you?

    b. How are the experiences of one of the characters you saw different from your own? How are they similar to yours?

    c. What is one thing you learned from watching this show?

3. Get personal with stories of racism. Both of us have seen what happens when those who are white encounter the stories of people of color in a way that opens their eyes to a new reality. For those of you who are white, we encourage you to learn about the realities of racism by hearing stories of its impact from brothers and sisters of color. Take the step of asking your friends of color whether they would feel comfortable sharing stories of when their racial and ethnic background has led to discrimination, prejudice, fear, or other ramifications so that you and your kids can learn from their experiences. Possible questions to ask include these:

    a. Have you ever experienced any negative incidents related to your race or ethnicity? Would you be willing to share about any of those incidents?

    b. How did you handle those incidents? What were the short- and long-term impacts for you?

    c. What do you wish people who don't have the same background knew about what it is like to walk in your particular racial or ethnic shoes?

4. During heritage months, commit to learning as a family about a historic or prominent person of color. Ask your kids to help select a key figure, assist with research, and report what is discovered. Here is a list of notable heritage months:

   a. Black History Month (February)
   b. Asian Pacific American Heritage Month (May)
   c. Jewish American Heritage Month (May)
   d. Hispanic Heritage Month
      (September 15–October 15)
   e. Native American Heritage Month (November)

5. Create regular family check-in times to talk about difficult topics. As your family begins to more proactively pursue education and conversations about race and racism, you and your kids alike might experience reactions such as denial, disorientation, shame, or even anger.[10] When those reactions occur, don't try to gloss over them or turn away from the discomfort. Instead, make space to share with your kids what you are feeling and learning, and encourage them to do the same during family devotions, over dinner, or before bedtime. It will be pivotal for them to witness you as their parent going through this uncomfortable process of learning and persevering nonetheless. By developing endurance rather than fostering fragility and by taking a posture of humility and openness, you can model effective ways to help eradicate racism.

6. Join the Be the Bridge Facebook group to listen and learn as you journey toward racial understanding. If you want to become more involved in antiracist activities, Be the Bridge (founded by Latasha Morrison in 2016) offers numerous resources and models for pursuing reconciliation work in community with other Christian brothers and sisters. For white readers in the beginning of this journey, they also have free resources to help you listen and

learn rather than move into "white savior" mode. Stay in a posture of cultural humility,[11] recognizing that you need to continue to submit to leaders of color in this area instead of positioning yourself as a newly enlightened antiracist activist. Your heart might be in the right place, but there is a time to listen and learn. There is also a time and a place to take action and raise your voice for what is right and just. But if you are a white person in the beginning stage of a journey toward understanding issues of race, James's admonition to be slow to speak is particularly relevant (James 1:19). (If you aren't on Facebook, you can find details on how to access these free resources in appendix 5.)

7. Offer the following prayer either in your own devotional time or with your family:

God, Our Heavenly Maker,
We confess the unkind, unloving ways we have treated other
humans. We submit our family to the Spirit's leading because we
know that, at the end of time, in the Day of the Lord, people from
every tongue, tribe, and nation will be gathered both to worship
you and to be judged by you for all we have done and all we have
left undone. We confess the North American church's sinful legacy
of contributing to racial injustices both large and small,
and we commit ourselves here and now to facing how this legacy
has kept many from understanding and embracing the true gospel
of Jesus Christ, who came to save the world from its sins. God,
strip our minds and our hearts of racist thoughts, words, and
actions. Use us as your hands and feet to dismantle racism in our
country, and lead us into greater obedience and love.
Amen.

Opening Our Hearts to Lament

It was March 16, 2021. I (Michelle) had just received a news alert about the Atlanta massacre in which eight people—six of whom were Asian women—were killed in shootings at three spas. A young white man and self-identified Christian, Robert Aaron Long, was responsible for all three shootings. Long yelled, "I'm going to kill all Asians!"[1] When he was finally caught by the police, he was headed to Florida, possibly planning to carry out more shootings.[2] As this information was streaming in, I began to weep. I had a visceral reaction to that news. It was the kind of news that made me nauseous, and I felt like I was barely able to move.

As I sat motionless, crumpled in a chair in my living room, my young son overheard my sobs and came running.

"Mama, why are you sad?" he asked.

It wasn't an easy question to answer. How much should I share with my five-year-old? How should I speak the truth about this situation without making it too heavy for my young child to bear? How could I put my thoughts into words simple enough for my son to understand?

It had already been a brutal year of escalating anti-Asian

racism because of the COVID-19 global pandemic.[3] In the early months of 2020, Asians were shouted at. As the year progressed and as fears of the coronavirus heightened, we were coughed on and spit on. It didn't take long before Asians were shoved and kicked. Then we were slashed, stabbed, and doused in acid. In 2020 and 2021, the Stop AAPI Hate reporting center cataloged over nine thousand incidents of anti-Asian racism, including a skyrocketing rate of hate crimes committed against elderly Asians.[4] I had already found myself on my living room couch countless times, weeping over the senselessness of this evil. The Atlanta massacre was but another tragedy in a long line of racialized crimes against the Asian American community.

I hugged my son tight and replied, "People like you and me were killed today."

After a short pause, he replied, "What should we do?"

It was a more profound question than I had expected of my child. What *should* Christians do in moments like this? The sad reality is that, in the wake of racial tragedies, many Christians choose to do nothing. When asked about racial pain and injustice in our country, 28 percent of practicing Christians say, "There's nothing the Church should do." Thirty-three percent of white practicing Christians select this option.[5] Making matters more complicated are the myriad voices that tend to blame the victim for his or her death.

However, that's not the response that my husband and I want our children to have. Whenever a racial tragedy happens in our country or somewhere in the world for that matter, our posture as a family is to first respond with lament. My family laments every time a life is lost because every person's life has value and meaning. Every person is made by God and in his image, and anyone's senseless death breaks God's heart. Our hearts, too, should feel that brokenness.

So, between sniffles and more tears, I turned off the television and began to pray with my son, asking God to comfort the victims' families. I prayed for God to bring justice and healing

> **Lament must be a core element of our Christian witness, and we can pass this value on to our children as we intentionally practice lament in our daily lives.**

to the Asian American community, and I finished by asking God to deal with the evils of this world and to comfort and protect those affected by this tragedy.

That moment together catalyzed something in my son. The next time our family heard about a racial tragedy, it was my son who first said, "We need to pray." Now it's become a rhythmic part of our family life. The sad reality is that racial tragedies will continue occurring in our country. My children know that, but even more importantly, they know that their first response as followers of Jesus should be to lament—to mourn with those who mourn and to cry out to God.

Integral to being a race-wise family is the choice to respond with open hearts of lament to the anger and pain that our country and our communities of color in particular feel deeply. Lament must be a core element of our Christian witness, and we can pass this value on to our children as we intentionally practice lament in our daily lives.

Defining Terms

There are two key stepping stones to developing a posture of lament: empathy and compassion. Let's unpack all three of these terms to better understand how they relate to and differ from one another.

Empathy is "the ability to recognize, understand, and share the thoughts and feelings of another person."[6] To empathize with someone requires us to exercise our imagination. We must step outside ourselves, including our own point of view, and put ourselves in someone else's shoes. Empathy isn't simply thinking to ourselves, *I wonder what that person is going through.* It's a posture that imaginatively transports us into someone else's world and considers how we might think or feel if we were experiencing the same joys or pains that he or she is. In this sense, empathy is not a mere intellectual exercise but a practice that seeks deep connection with another person. It's the ability to hug a friend or stranger alike, cry with that person, and say, "I know. I understand what you're going through right now. I'm here."

Sadly, most of us are not as empathetic as we should be. In fact, in our age of technology and consumerism, empathy is on the decline. According to neuroscientist Jamil Zaki, "in one study, the average American college student in 2009 scored as less empathic than 75 percent of students in 1979. This suggests our care is eroding."[7] Belinda Bauman, author of *Brave Souls: Experiencing the Audacious Power of Empathy*, noted, "Empathy as a *practice* is declining. Researchers call this the 'empathy gap,' with some saying it is heading toward extinction." She went on to say, "For too long, we've dismissed empathy as irrelevant and contradictory to faith, when in fact it's an essential biblical concept that offers us a gateway to the change we seek."[8]

There are several factors causing the erosion of empathy. One factor is social separation. The less proximate we are to real people with real needs, the less we care about their suffering and pain. Some of us live in monocultural neighborhoods or attend monocultural churches, which in and of themselves aren't bad, but these spaces can inhibit our knowledge of and engagement with people who are different from us. Social media can also make us socially disconnected. Teenagers who use social media frequently, for example, are more than three times as likely to feel socially isolated.[9] In an age when we have digital access to everything at the tips of our fingers, we are more distanced from one another than ever before. This lack of proximity is catalyzing not just the erosion of empathy but the erosion of compassion as well.

> **Compassion is caught, not taught.**

Compassion is the "sympathetic consciousness of others' distress together with a desire to alleviate it."[10] When you are compassionate, you recognize or feel the pain of another, and then you do your best to alleviate the person's suffering. Compassion thus involves a tangible expression of love for and solidarity with those who are suffering.[11]

Compassion literally means "to suffer with." In the Bible, Jesus modeled what it looks like to be a co-sufferer. For example, in John 11:33–35, when he went to the grave of Lazarus and saw his friends weeping, Jesus wept with them. But that's not all he did. After mourning with those who mourn, Jesus then pursued healing and restoration for the hurting by raising Lazarus from the dead. Being compassionate means we care about helping people. Being compassionate just means that we emotionally connect first, and we pursue tangible, physical solutions second. Jesus stayed present in a moment of communal pain. He didn't run away from suffering, he didn't feel overwhelmed by suffering, nor did he pretend suffering didn't exist. We must do likewise. Compassion is an attribute of God (Psalm 86:15) and is to be a core quality of God's people (1 Peter 3:8).

In our (Michelle's) home, we have a daily saying: "Show God's love." To care about suffering in the world isn't a secular agenda. Rather, it reflects the heart of God. God first empathized with us and showed compassion to us. Therefore, we must empathize and show compassion to others. It's not always easy for us adults—let alone for our children—to be compassionate. But when we ground ourselves in God's character and seek to love the world the way he does, we can pray, "God, we need your empathy today. God, help us be more compassionate like you." Moreover, the more we as parents can model this in our own lives, the more our children will be able to see the heart of God in action. Compassion is usually caught, not taught.

Lament is broadly defined as "grieving for the present situation yet acting in the hopeful assurance that God will deliver and redeem."[12] New Testament scholar Rebekah Eklund said that lament is "a persistent cry for salvation to the God who promises to save, in a situation of suffering or sin, in the confident hope that this God hears and responds to cries, and acts *now* and *in the future* to make whole."[13]

The persistent cry for salvation is found in the book of Psalms. Almost half of the songs are laments, pleas amid despair and suffering for divine intervention and help. The psalms of lament follow a pattern we can learn from. By studying biblical prayers and songs of lament, we learn how to express the depths of our emotions, and we can pass these lessons on to our children. Lament involves

- crying out to God
- asking for help
- responding with trust

Learning how to lament can help us teach our children how to come to the Lord with both their sorrows and the sorrows of others. When they experience or witness loss, disappointment, injustice, and fear, they can cry out to God, following the pattern of the biblical laments.

A Biblical Case for Lament

It's easy to teach our children to thank God for the many blessings in their lives. If we have a relatively privileged existence— if we don't live in poverty, if we have a roof over our heads and some disposable income—it's easy to emphasize celebration and praise in our homes. Our prayers at mealtimes focus on thanking God for our day, for good food, friends, and opportunities. The songs we sing to our children as we tuck them into bed center on God's love and joy. The Bible stories we read tend to highlight the heroic deeds of people long ago, God's intervention that leads to victory, and how everything works out at the end of the day.

Of course, praising God and celebrating the good things in our lives isn't wrong. These expressions of worship and thankfulness have their proper place in the Christian faith. But a praise-only focus will prevent us from making space for lament.

How often does your family spend time in communal lament? Do your children participate in practices of lament at your church or around your family dinner table? When was the last time your family wept together and cried out to God because of the evil in this world? Sadly, many of us turn to lament only in moments of personal crisis. Expression of lament isn't part of many families' regular conversations and prayers—and when it is, we tend to focus on our own troubles, not the troubles of others.

You could argue that the modern Christian family doesn't know how to lament. Cries of grief and protest have faded from our daily rhythms of faith in large part because the Christianity we've been taught by the American church avoids lament. Theologian Soong-Chan Rah explained that American Christian worship emphasizes celebration because the majority of Anglo-American Christians and churches are middle class and enjoy a certain level of privilege and comfort. In other words, majority-culture Christians "interpret the Christian tradition through a lens of prosperity and praise."[14] In his book *Prophetic Lament*, Rah wrote, "Christian communities arising from celebration do not want their lives changed, because their lives are in a good place."[15]

However, God's Word reminds us both of our deep need to lament and of the requirement to teach one another and our children how to do the same. Jeremiah 9:20 states,

> You women, hear the word of the LORD;
> open your ears to the words of his mouth.
> Teach your daughters how to wail;
> teach one another a lament.

We are called, as parents, to teach our children how to wail. Not just in times of personal crisis but for the suffering of the world—for the people in our communities who haven't been treated equally, for every instance of racial profiling and racial prejudice, for the trauma and mental health struggles that so many people within subdominant cultures now face. For Black and Brown people shot down in the street. Being a race-wise family means raising children who are aware of the broken realities of race in the world around them and who, to paraphrase philosopher and political activist Cornel West, *let suffering speak.*[16]

In Scripture, we see that God longs for his children to cry out to him. God himself shows that anger toward injustice is appropriate (Psalm 7:11). Too often, hurting minorities are dismissed for expressing their emotions, and families of every ethnicity must learn how to make space for these complex emotions. As individuals, as families, and even as a church, we should make space for people's cries of pain, legitimize them, and recognize that God calls us to freely express our pain and, when we hear such cries, to respond with compassionate care.

To begin learning how to listen to suffering and respond as a family, we need to open our Bibles together and spend time reading and reflecting on biblical lament. The best first step we can take is gaining helpful and appropriate language for lament. Too often in our world today, lament is equated to complaining. However, lament in the Bible—including in Job, Lamentations, and Psalms—is simply grieving. Biblical lament takes the form of both verbal and physical sorrow and it is offered up to God with the hope that he will deliver and redeem.[17]

Consider, for example, Psalm 102:1–2. In this prayer, you hear the psalmist's frustration that God doesn't feel present:

> Hear my prayer, LORD;
>> let my cry for help come to you.
> Do not hide your face from me
>> when I am in distress.

Turn your ear to me;
    when I call, answer me quickly.

First, the psalmist begged God to be visibly present and not hide his face. Then the psalmist asked God to respond to his current suffering by turning his ear to him. This psalm is deeply relatable. When we personally are suffering or we feel overwhelmed by the suffering in the world, we often wonder where God is and if he can hear us. The psalmist in Psalm 102 felt the same. However, he cried out to God and expressed those emotions with the hope and even assurance that God would come and God would answer. So we can read Psalm 102 to our children and say, "Let's ask God to comfort us with his presence and to hear our cries for help."

In Psalm 42 we find a model for articulating confusion when we're in pain:

My tears have been my food
    day and night,
while people say to me all day long,
    "Where is your God?"
These things I remember
    as I pour out my soul:
how I used to go to the house of God
    under the protection of the Mighty One
with shouts of joy and praise
    among the festive throng. (verses 3–4)

Andrew Williams argued that the psalmist here was struggling with depression.[18] Not only was he unable to sleep because of his grief, but his community and friends shamed him, implying that something was wrong with him if God seemed far away. The psalmist himself was wrestling with the possible truth of their words and also remembering better times: he used to go to the house of the God with shouts of joy and praise. His plight doesn't sound too different from the faithful believer who stops attending church during a mental health struggle. Yet the psalmist didn't quit. He persevered by bringing to God both his current reality and his memories. He offered up his fears and doubts, believing that God would renew his spirit. It's okay to not be able to make sense of your pain. When we—or our children—are hurting, it's okay to simply pray, "God, I don't even understand my own emotions, but I know you do. Help me."

Biblical lament also teaches us that prayers and other expressions of sorrow and pain are important not just in our faith but for humanity. The psalmists in the Bible didn't merely list personal struggles. They bemoaned the problems so that their entire community or nation heard. As followers of Jesus and especially as families, we are to be mindful of the pain and injustice in our own lives *and in* the lives of others. Lament was always meant to be expressed in community. We were created to talk about the shadows of life in one another's presence and to be both speakers and hearers of painful truths—and this is a posture of heart that we want to cultivate early and often in our children.

What if we parents strive to read psalms of lament with our children and teach them to call on God to be true to his character and to keep his promises? Our family rhythms must make space for both joy and lament. We must help our children see that trusting God doesn't mean the absence of pain and despair.

Many Christian families and churches have wrongly concluded that "lament is unnecessary if one trusts, loves, and obeys God."[19] Perhaps you were taught something similar growing up. In some Christian homes, children are taught "Don't be sad. Just trust God." Perhaps you heard your own parents say something like "Stop complaining and just pray." Though these sentiments can be well intentioned, they fall short

> **We must help our children see that trusting God doesn't mean the absence of pain and despair.**

of truly valuing the expression of a wide range of emotions to God. Lament isn't just a cry for attention or a cheap way to play the race card. In fact, when we choose such wrong thinking, we refuse to see that lament is a biblical exercise that helps us better understand both the dark realities of this world and the compassionate heart of our sovereign God.[20] Lament is an opportunity for followers of Jesus to show a watching world the sacred practice of drawing near to God when the darkness of evil and injustice is at our doors.

What Lament Does to the Heart

Lament helps us slow down to become more aware of and in tune with the suffering around us. Here are three ways in which lament changes our hearts for the better.

Lament Moves Us Beyond Dismissiveness

We are often quick to deny or minimize the pain that people of color experience in their everyday lives. Asian Americans who talk about their experiences of racism during COVID-19 are called snowflakes.[21] The Black community cries out after the murder of a Black man by armed white civilians, and evangelicals question whether the victim is to blame.[22] After the murder of George Floyd, people were quick to talk about Black-on-Black crime and whether Floyd had a criminal record instead of mourning the loss of a fellow image bearer.[23] Native Americans plead to have conversations about difficult topics such as their stolen land, and we just turn a blind eye.[24] The news reports flash images of children in cages at the border and tell stories of young immigrant girls having forced hysterectomies at detention centers, and we go about our day without taking a second to grieve.[25]

Instead of actually hearing the outcries of our friends and

neighbors of color, many Christians convince themselves that conversations about race are lies or, at the very least, are exaggerated and misconstrued. Leaders tell their churches that current problems of race are secular threats infiltrating the church.[26] Meanwhile, our children sit by us while we watch the nightly news and hear us mutter insensitive comments about "all Black people" or "all Asians" or "all Latinos." But we respond this way only when things aren't personal. We figure that if it's not happening in our lives, it must not be true.

Lament counters this instinct. It challenges us to hear someone's story of pain and believe that it's true. It teaches us to say, "Wow. I'm so sorry. Please tell me more. I want to understand" instead of "You're just making this up. I'm sick and tired of hearing about these things." When we value lament as a practice, the posture of our families will be to lean in instead of pull back. Moreover, as Soong-Chan Rah argued, "If we believe in the necessity of prophetic lament, we wouldn't so easily dismiss the call to understand the need for #blacklivesmatter and [would] not so easily move to all lives matter."[27]

Lament Softens Our Hearts and Teaches Us How to Mourn

The more we make space to hear other people's cries, the more our hearts should soften to their pain. We may never fully understand what someone else is going through, but that's not the point. When we choose to listen and lean in, our hearts and souls transform so that we *desire* to "mourn with those who mourn" (Romans 12:15).

I (Helen) recall a time when my church family was rocked by the news that a youth from a low-income neighborhood in Chicago who was connected to one of our partner ministries had been shot in the face. He'd always had a smile on his face and been a part of numerous cross-ministry youth events, and he knew many adults and kids in my church, so our community was in shock and saddened when we heard about the incident.

> **We must not fully shield our children from the problems of race in our world.**

All we could do while waiting to hear about his status was to pray. As the youth pastor led us in an honest and tearful expression of anxiety, fear, and sorrow, I felt my own tears fall and could hear the sniffles of others throughout the church who were joining in heartfelt prayers for God to heal this young man. Gun violence in Chicago was no longer something distant on the news; it had become a deeply personal issue that the congregation needed to lament together.

Communal lament is about solidarity. We must be willing to dwell with those who are crying to the Lord in sorrow and anger and collectively wait for the Lord's deliverance. We can also learn from others whose communities have more experience holding and responding to deep pain. Many modern-day Koreans and Korean Americans, for example, are familiar with the concept of *han*, the deep communal suffering in response to the hardships that Korea has been through. These include the Japanese colonization and the division of Korea into two countries, which has resulted in the deaths or separation of so many Korean family members, my (Helen's) extended family included. African Americans, Native Americans, and other marginalized groups share a deep legacy of suffering and lament because of many generations of abuse and inhumane treatment. In a posture of solidarity, the church can listen to and learn from communities such as these, not glossing over any expressed pain and sorrow but grieving and lamenting alongside our brothers and sisters when opportunities present themselves.

This proposal will go against the instinct many of us have to shield our children from the evils of this world. It can be uncomfortable to see and hear the cries of a wailing person. Sometimes we don't know how to make space for a person in pain or, worse, we don't believe their pain is valid. Other times, we worry that our children may lose their innocence if we pull back the curtain. We want them to be happy, not weighed down by the problems of this world. But even that perspective is born of privilege. It assumes your day-to-day life is relatively care-free and ignores that many families around the world are forced to confront racial suffering firsthand. For many children, the problems of racism *are* their daily reality. Solidarity begins by making space for the cries of other people, listening to their pain, and learning to mourn with them. This is why we must not fully shield our children from the problems of race in our world. We can address those issues in age-appropriate ways be-cause the alternative for our children—being ignorant of racial inequality and systemic injustice and refusing to care about or be moved by other people's suffering—is much worse.

Lament Empowers Us to Long for a Different Reality

Lament helps us become dissatisfied with racism and racial pain. Instead of touting the line "That's just the way things are," we mourn with those who mourn, knowing that within Christ's kingdom these injustices shouldn't be.

This last aspect of lament is a culmination of the first two: once we lean in to listen and learn and once we truly open our hearts to mourn with those who mourn, we must take action. Lament should travel from our heads and hearts to our hands. Our expres-sions of grief and sorrow must move from verbal cries to the Lord to tangible actions such as protesting the evils of racism and raising our voices in civic spaces. We need to turn lament into activism.

> **Lament should travel from our heads and hearts to our hands. We need to turn lament into activism.**

Practices to Cultivate Empathy, Compassion, and Lament as a Race-Wise Family

Oh, to imagine a new generation that laments one another's pain. What if our children's generation could commit to mourning with those who mourn? How different our world might become! Instead of marginalizing and sidelining others, instead of dismissing and silencing others, let's encourage our children to forge new paths of communal lament and compassion. It starts in each of our homes, and here are nine ways to begin setting a new legacy:

1. Print out a feeling chart or create a feeling wheel with your children. You can google "Feeling chart" or "Feeling wheel" for examples. The different emotions should include *happy, sad, confused, angry, nervous, frustrated,* etc. Once a day, find time to sit down with your kids and ask them, "How are you feeling today?" This is also a helpful exercise to practice right after a racial incident at school or in the news. Encourage your children to express their emotions by pointing to the chart and then have a conversation about it.

2. Read books on every emotion, from sadness to anger to compassion, so that your children have emotional tool kits to express those emotions in the face of racial injustice (see our suggested list of books in appendix 3).

3. When reading the Bible together, regularly ask questions like "What do you think this person felt when that happened?" or "Whom do you most identify with in this passage? Why?"

4. Help your children make the connection between suffering and specific people in your own community. For example, sit down and identify all the people your family knows who are going through particularly difficult trials, such as families of color who have experienced racial

othering or witnessed racism in their own lives and on a national stage. Name specific challenges for Black Americans when yet another incident of police brutality occurs, pray for migrant children who may yet be stuck at our nation's border, or reach out to leaders in the Asian American or Native American community to better understand their experiences and needs. Then print pictures of each family (if appropriate), pray daily for them, and send them words or pictures of encouragement.

5. Make lament part of daily prayer in your home. At the dinner table, during family devotions, or right before bed, pray about the injustices in this world and ask God to open your hearts to mourn with those who mourn. Don't be afraid to let your children see you grieve over what is happening in our world. The times that our kids see us in tears because of ongoing racial violence will perhaps have an even greater impact than any words we could say about it.

6. Model healthy grief before your children. When someone you know is sick or passes away, make space to grieve as a family and as a community. Also, show your children the importance of just sitting with people who are grieving. Have no other agenda than to show solidarity with them in their pain. Consider adopting a ritual similar to or inspired by the Jewish practice of sitting shiva, which is the seven-day mourning period after a loved one has passed away to allow immediate family members to grieve together and spend time with others who come to express their condolences. This practice will challenge our westernized comfort zones, but this is how we grieve loss together.

7. Practice not getting defensive. You can do this with your own kids first. When they get angry, don't shut them down with a knee-jerk reaction. The way they are treated when they have strong emotions is how they will in turn treat others with strong emotions.

8. Intentionally seek to listen to and learn from those who have stories of trauma and pain to share. For example, serve at a local refugee nonprofit, a homeless shelter, or a pregnancy resource center. Part of how we learn to mourn is by hearing regularly about the pain and trauma of other communities. Our children must be exposed to a world vastly different from—and often more broken than—our own.

9. Become part of or create spaces for communal lament. See whether your church can start a regular night of lament. Host a regular night of communal prayer and lament in your home and invite people of other cultures to lead it.

10. Offer the following prayer either in your own devotional time or with your family:

God of Lament,
We long for a new generation that mourns one another's pain.
Soften our own hearts. Instead of marginalizing and sidelining
others, instead of dismissing and silencing others, may our family
forge new paths of communal lament and compassion. Oh, how
different our world might become! God, motivate us as parents to
intentionally read psalms of lament with our children and teach
them to call on you at all times. May the rhythms of our family
make space for both joy and lament. May our children understand
that trusting you doesn't result in the absence of pain and despair.
We can begin a new legacy in our home and in our community.
God, help us lament.
Amen.

Posture Five

Speaking Words of Love and Truth

"HEY, POCAHONTAS! OVER HERE, POCAHONTAS!"

A group of children swarmed around me (Michelle) in the school gym, chanting these words and preventing me from getting to my next class. Their taunts were accompanied by caricatured hand and body movements that imitated Native American culture—or at least what these children thought was a representation of Native American culture.

I stood there, silent, petrified. I wasn't sure if I should try to run for the gym door. The kids circling me were getting closer. Their behavior felt violent. I certainly didn't want to make things worse.

The school bell finally came to my rescue. As a hall monitor neared and the kids dispersed, I crumpled to the floor in tears. This wasn't the first time I had been racially bullied. Not only that, but I had been racially misidentified as well. Though I am a second-generation Indian American, my classmates were teasing me for being a Native American. Their taunts were racially insensitive—and wrong.

My classmates' words rocked my confidence. For months afterward, I internalized an overwhelming feeling of shame about who I was and about the color of my skin, and I started to think that nobody liked me or wanted to be my friend.

This is the power that words have.

As parents, we need to understand that the words we say—and, by extension, the words our children say—are either adding to the racial chaos around us or healing it. There is a pervasive myth that children are unaware of and unaffected by racist rhetoric,[1] but research has shown the ways in which damaging words and ideas—whether heard from parents, media, or classmates—trickle down into the classroom and playground. As a result, young children speak racist rhetoric that they themselves may not even fully understand.

In our country today, for instance, Asians are repeatedly asked, "Where are you from?" or told, "Go back to your country"—words that reinforce the idea that Asians are foreigners and even foreign threats.[2] Many believe in the myth of the dangerous immigrant. Forty-two percent of Americans think that immigrants make crime worse in the United States.[3] People who don't speak English (or don't speak it well) are mocked—even by national leaders—and seen as less intelligent. Many immigrants who come to this country work seven days a week and don't have time to study English. However, the expectation that they understand and speak English perfectly—often enforced in workplaces, schools, and even churches—can make immigrants feel uneducated and dumb. Ethnic foods are located in separate aisles in grocery stores and often not seen as American. Worse, children who bring homemade food from other cultures often have their foods labeled as smelly and gross in the school cafeteria (both of us as well as our children have experienced this). The Black community is labeled as crime ridden or the bad part of town.[4] Many of these ideas have been perpetuated for centuries in our country, and they hold considerable power today. We should never forget that our children are listening and being formed by what they hear. We have a great privilege and responsibility to train our children to speak words of love and truth, especially when it comes to issues of

> **We must look to Scripture to tell us what words we need to learn and unlearn and to teach us how to do this well.**

race. But it's going to take work.

It's not easy to speak affirming language over ourselves and one another. It's much easier to focus on one another's flaws and on the things that bother us about other people, especially people of other cultures. It's often easier to see the problems rather than the beauty. Not only that, but many of us have also absorbed harmful ideas and stories about other people such that we verbalize inappropriate ideas on race without even realizing it. We need to slow down and consider our words carefully.

This chapter equips race-wise families to understand why we shouldn't say racially harmful words. It also provides a guide for using positive, biblical language related to race and culture. These words might look slightly different from one decade to the next. Our language is always evolving, but one thing we know for certain: words matter. We must look to Scripture to tell us what words we need to learn and unlearn and to teach us how to do this well.

Defining Terms

There is nothing wrong with the name *Pocahontas* in and of itself, but the kids were using this name for me (Michelle) as a racial slur. A **racial slur** is biased, hurtful, and offensive language based on a person's ethnicity or culture. Racial slurs exist everywhere, from the schoolyard to the workplace, as graffiti on walls, buildings, and streets, and as comments in our social media feeds.

Moreover, racial slurs like this one are born out of race-based stereotypes. A **race-based stereotype** is an oversimplified story about a group of people based on generalizations, limited interactions, and hearsay.[5] People often say they don't believe stereotypes about other races, cultures, or ethnicities, but they might still believe *stories* they've learned about people. False narratives about people of different skin colors or people who immigrate to our country can influence us in ways we may not even realize.

Finally, **racial prejudices** typically arise from race-based stereotypes. *The American Heritage Dictionary* provides these two meanings for the term: "an adverse judgment or opinion formed unfairly or without knowledge of the facts" and "irrational suspicion or hatred of a particular social group, such as a race or the adherents of a religion."[6]

Loving God and Loving Others Through Our Words

Training our children to speak kind and loving words to people of different ethnicities and skin tones begins with heart formation. As Luke 6:45 says, "The mouth speaks what the heart is full of." Children speak affirming language to their neighbors and friends out of love for them. Our children must love people as full-bodied humans and as cultural image bearers because when they love others for whom God made them to be, our children's attitudes, words, and actions will reflect that love. This is what happens when we fully understand and seek to live out the command to love God and love others. If we care about the words our families speak about race to people of other ethnicities and cultures, then our first focus must be on raising children to love God and love others in all they do and say.

Throughout Scripture, we see people holding prejudices against others based on their skin color or on factors such as their ethnicity or dialect (Judges 12). Consider the prophetess Miriam, who spoke out against Moses's wife. Numbers 12 states that she "spoke against Moses because of the Cushite woman whom he had married (for he had indeed married a Cushite woman)" (verse 1, NRSV). Old Testament professor J. Daniel

Hays wrote that *Cush* "is used regularly to refer to the area south of Egypt, above the cataracts on the Nile, where a Black African civilization flourished for over two thousand years. Thus it is quite clear that Moses marries a Black African woman."[7] Miriam might have been prejudiced against this woman because of her darker skin. Miriam held no love for her and made it evident in her complaint. But God made it immediately clear that this kind of language wasn't acceptable. He himself had never criticized Moses's wife or their interracial marriage; Miriam shouldn't have either. So God punished Miriam with leprosy. It's almost as if he were saying to her, "So, you value lighter skin? Well, now I'll make you as white as a leper." It was a punishment that fit the crime.

Ethnic divisions continued into the New Testament era, and we read about full-on hatred between Greeks, Jews, Samaritans, Scythians, and barbarians. It's this world of racial hostility that Jesus entered and offered a different way forward. Throughout his life and ministry, he made it abundantly clear that he doesn't tolerate negative, demeaning language between ethnic groups. In fact, he called out xenophobic rhetoric even among his own disciples. In Luke 9:51–56, Jesus and his disciples wanted to visit a Samaritan village. They sent messengers ahead to get things ready for their arrival, but the Samaritans refused to welcome Jesus. The disciples, enraged, asked him whether they could call fire down and destroy them all. But Jesus rebuked them. He doesn't allow those who follow him to use violent words or treat people of other ethnicities in a violent manner. This kind of hostility has no place in the family of God. It's certainly not the way of love.

Jesus declared that people will know we are Christians by our love (John 13:35). The way of love is the better way to which Jesus calls those who follow him. He challenges people over and over again to love those who are different from them—to go over and above in loving them, in fact. Consider the ways that Jesus addressed people he met. He called them "child of God," "son," and "daughter"—terms that express his affection

> **Jesus's words offered both physical and spiritual healing, and our words can do the same.**

for people. More than that, it is familial language, inviting us into the family of God. In other words, when Jesus spoke to people, he loved them, pointed them to himself, and invited them to be part of his family. Jesus's words offered both physical and spiritual healing, and our words can do the same.

Like Proverbs 16:24 says, "Gracious words are a honeycomb, sweet to the soul and healing to the bones." Positive, proactive words have the power to heal. We can begin breaking cycles of racism and ethnic division by choosing to speak words of love, affirmation, and truth instead of insult and condescension. The body of Christ is called to "not let any unwholesome talk come out of your mouths, but only what is helpful for building others up according to their needs, that it may benefit those who listen" (Ephesians 4:29). As believers, both individually and corporately, we need to learn how to encourage one another and build one another up with our words (1 Thessalonians 5:11). This is a fundamental part of how we love God and love *all* our neighbors.

We recognize that children can love God and still speak hurtful words, not out of cruelty—although that is sometimes the case—but out of ignorance. Kids just go along with other kids sometimes without realizing the harm they are doing. Nevertheless, this is all the more reason that parents have to take the initiative to help their kids know what *not* to say. Many of us may assume our kids would never say damaging words about kids (or adults) of other cultures, but that is a dangerous assumption. We can't just do nothing and hope for the best. We are

> **We are called to pursue a posture of love as a family and to choose to speak positive words.**

called to pursue a posture of love as a family and to choose to speak positive words.

This begins with us. If we as parents aren't modeling words of love, our lessons to our children on this subject won't have the same formational effect. We need to learn how to speak love in heated conversations about race (not to mention as a general way of life). We need to cultivate hearts of love so that we can speak humbly and respectfully with our neighbors and coworkers of other ethnicities and cultures. We need to ask God to instill in us his deep love and then teach our kids to ask for the same. The more they see us speaking lovingly in everyday conversations, the more they will learn how to do so themselves, whether they're talking to a sibling, a neighbor, or a classmate with a different skin tone.

Embracing the Prophetic and Pastoral Voices

The practices of calling out and calling in are what we refer to as the prophetic voice and the pastoral voice, respectively. As Christian families, we need to develop both of these voices if we are going to both call out racially harmful words—in ourselves and in others—*and* replace these harmful words with words of truth and love.

Prophetically Speak Truth in Love

Speaking truth in love includes standing up for those being insulted and maligned because of their ethnicity, skin color, or culture. Perhaps you've heard someone make a joke about race or make fun of the way someone talks, the way she dresses, or her physical appearance. Perhaps someone you know has made an angry comment about Asian people, immigrants, or poverty. Perhaps you've heard someone make assumptions about the kinds of foods, preferences, or mindsets that a person has, whether or not he belongs to a particular ethnic group, where he's from, how rich or poor he is, how he should talk or act, or what kind of job he should have. These harmful, reductive ways of speaking about other cultures in no way communicate love for those people or people groups.

The next time you or your children hear someone make a comment about an entire people group by saying something like "All Black people do this," "All white people do this," or "All immigrants are like this," address it. You can say something as simple as "That's a stereotype, and it's simply not true. We should never generalize about an entire people group." You can also encourage that person to keep his or her comments nuanced by saying, "I met an immigrant who . . ." or "I knew one white person who said . . ."

We should never try to guess a person's cultural identity. Instead, teach your children to give people the honor of self-definition. Terms like *Black* and *African American*, *Native American* and *First Nation*, *Latino*, *Hispanic*, *South Asian*, *East Asian*, and *desi* all have different implications for people's ethnic and cultural identities. Each of us has a unique way of describing our skin tone, and honoring one another's aesthetic diversity means making our different colors visible but not hypervisible. Categories are even more complicated for bicultural and multicultural individuals. Some people are half Asian and half Black or half Chicano and half Asian. We should never assume that someone's phenotype (physical characteristics) is a direct giveaway of his or her ethnicity. Don't guess. Teach your children not to ask people, "What are you?" or "Where are you from?" Rather, model questions such as "What are your ethnic roots?" and "Can you tell me about your culture?"

This goes without saying, but as a family you should never use or justify racist rhetoric. Racist rhetoric includes calling someone the N-word or "a wetback" as well as using terms that include skin colors and ethnicities such as "lazy Mexican" or "angry Black woman." If you ever catch yourself or your children using words like these, take a moment to pause and then commit to not saying those words again because they don't show God's love. Also, actively seek to replace these kinds of words with affirming language about ethnicity and culture. We should never feel satisfied with saying words that are barely civil. It's not simply about not causing a fight or not saying something insulting or racist. We must strive to speak words full of love and the power to restore what has been tainted and lost.

Develop a Pastoral Voice

The pastoral voice is positive, biblical language on race that points people to Christ and makes them feel loved. For example, if your children are interested in talking about skin color with their friends, it should be done in a way that values people (for example, linking ethnic distinctions to discussions of cultural traditions and values). To this end, they can ask open-ended questions like "What's your story?" "What are you passionate about?" and "What's your family like?"

It's also important to compliment people's appearance and dress without actually causing insult. If your child has straight hair and she is enamored by a friend's curly hair, teach her not to touch it. She should learn to say something like "I love your hair" while not crossing that person's boundaries. Compliments should never have qualifiers or comparisons like "You look nice for a Black woman" or "I love your skin tone. You're not as dark as *other* Indians I know." Additionally, we should refer to people by their names, not by what they look like. For example, instead of introducing someone by saying, "This is my Asian friend Jane" or "This is my Black friend Corey," just say, "This is my friend Jane" or "This is my friend Corey."

If kids want to compare themselves with each other, we should channel that toward shared likes and dislikes. Encourage your children to have conversations with their friends, classmates, or neighbors that are guided by questions such as

"What do you like?" and "What do you dislike?" They can talk about food, sports, hobbies, television shows, songs, games, and more. Encourage them to find out what they have in common and build bonds this way.

Practices to Speak Words of Love and Truth as a Race-Wise Family

The journey to becoming everyday speakers of love and truth requires us to thoughtfully consider what words we need to learn and unlearn. Affirmations help create positive feelings and actions. Proverbs 12:18 tells us that "thoughtless words can wound as deeply as any sword, but wisely spoken words can heal" (GNT). The more we speak kind, loving words to others, the more our words will generate kind, loving relationships. Choose kindness. Practice humility and thoughtfulness with your words. Work on cultivating a posture of love and truth in your family so that loving hearts and minds will flow into loving words for all. In this way, you each will be prepared to say something positive and proactive in difficult situations. We—both parents and children—need to reassess our vocabulary and consider what words we need to add or remove. Here are five practices to help you on this journey:

1. Sit down as a family and discuss the people of other cultures you rub shoulders with on a regular basis. How would you describe the health of these cross-cultural relationships? Do you feel like these relationships are centered by love? Would these people feel that you are a loving person?
2. When you invite a friend or family of another culture over to your house, tell them you want to listen to them and learn their point of view. Ask them whether they would be comfortable sharing how they describe themselves and what they wish people were saying—or would

stop saying—right now about issues related to ethnicity, culture, and race.

3. Encourage your children to write affirmations for themselves. Brainstorm positive, wonderful words they could use to describe themselves, either by making a bulleted list or by drawing and describing a self-portrait. Then write affirmations for a friend, classmate, or neighbor of a different ethnicity. If your children are young, write these affirmations for them. Share them aloud. Hang these words up somewhere as a reminder of the way God made you and others. Speak them over your family when you're experiencing something challenging or need to make a good choice.

4. If you do use words that hurt someone of a different ethnicity, in addition to apologizing to that person, tell your children about the experience so you can model how we are to behave when we err in this area. We must be humble and know when to apologize because we're not always right, even when we think we're being sensitive and appropriate. We must always consider how we can do better next time. Teach this process to your children. As a family, commit to being quick to apologize and ask for forgiveness, saying to the person you've hurt, "I care about you, and I'm sorry that my words hurt you. Will you forgive me?"

5. Take time at the dinner table and in one-on-one conversations with your children to discuss these questions: How can you speak truth to and over your friends of different skin tones? What are ways you can speak up when you see someone being mistreated? How can you speak love and truth to kids of other ethnicities who are mean to you? Empower your children to be brave and to fight for love and truth even when no one around them does.

6. Offer the following prayer either in your own devotional time or with your family:

God of Love and Truth,

Guide our steps as we begin a journey to becoming everyday speakers of love and truth. Slow down our thoughts, our emotions, and our bodies so that we may respectfully consider which words we need to learn and unlearn. Give us courage and strength to prophetically call out unkind and even evil words when we hear them. Give us humility to apologize when we ourselves have spoken harmful words. Give us compassion and love to pastorally point people to you and to speak soft words that are a balm to aching hearts.

Amen.

Responding to Current Events

I (MICHELLE) REMEMBER a fateful day back in grad school. It was a Sunday afternoon, and I had been invited to a local church gathering for lunch and a few games. The television was on in the background, and when the football game ended, the show segued to headline news with an update on the current immigration crisis. The reporter talked about incoming immigrants and their struggles in the US, including the fact that many don't speak English.

Of course, this situation wasn't a surprise to me. My own mother is part of the Indian diaspora and an immigrant to the US. My boyfriend (now husband), Aaron, and his family are immigrants from Mexico. Many of his relatives still don't speak English. Both Aaron and I grew up around aunts and uncles who spoke *only* Spanish or Gujarati. So as I watched the news coverage, I felt empathy for the current wave of people trying to navigate life in a new land.

This sentiment, however, wasn't shared by the other church members present. In fact, a young girl, perhaps twelve or thirteen years old, pretended to respond to the reporter by saying loudly for all to hear, "What did you expect? Dumb Mexicans."

Many of the adults and children around her laughed. The couple sitting next to my husband and me turned to smile at us, but their expression quickly changed when they saw our faces. Though they hadn't initially found the girl's statement offensive, it dawned on them at that moment that it may have offended us.

It wasn't only what the girl said that was troubling. Equally surprising to Aaron and me was her awareness of one of the biggest conversations happening in our country. So many of our kids today have greater access to news than ever before. Smartphones and viral content make it easy for kids to find videos of a Black man strangled by police officers or of children caged at the border. "Whether from social media accounts, conversations with peers or caregivers, overheard conversations, or the distress they witness in the faces of those they love, children know what is going on," California pediatrician Rhea Boyd said.[1] More than that, children are forming opinions about current events. The question, however, is, Are those opinions objective and kind?

In the living room that day, there was a quick hush, and the woman next to Aaron said, "I'm so sorry if that comment bothered you." My husband and I both nodded and said, "Thanks." But I didn't feel any better. It wasn't a real apology to begin with. It wasn't "I'm sorry this young girl said what she said. It was wrong." It was more like "I'm sorry you heard that."

No one corrected the girl. Her own parents had laughed at her joke. In fact, that news outlet has been known for making unkind remarks about immigrants, including calling them "an invasion" and "a replacement."[2] We've seen conservative television news imply that brown-skinned foreigners—coming to our country to escape unimaginable evils and now navigating a new language, new customs, and new people—are either nothing more than criminals or easy targets for cruel jokes. However, left-wing news networks are just as culpable. We've watched as a progressive channel made headlines for its appropriation of Mexican heritage and use of false stereotypes.

> **We must equip
> and empower our
> children to interpret race-
> related realities through
> a biblical lens.**

Christian families who lean left are just as capable of repeating unkind remarks about immigrants and people of color as conservatives. In fact, in their discussion of issues ranging from police brutality to missing indigenous women and girls, systemic racism, mass incarceration, educational inequity, anti-Asian racism, gentrification, and other modern configurations of segregation, both conservative and progressive news organizations can stigmatize racialized minorities in different ways, and their views trickle down to us, shaping our families' biases and assumptions.

It is crucial for a race-wise family to form healthy, holistic perspectives on current events, taking into account differing viewpoints as well as a person's or people group's humanity. Both we and our children need to gain a form of news literacy that is gospel driven. We must equip and empower our children to interpret race-related realities through a biblical lens. When it comes to current events, our goal should be to develop our children's critical thinking skills and biblical discernment so that they can respond to events in this world with both love and understanding.

Defining Terms

Theologian Karl Barth famously said, "Take your Bible and take your newspaper, and read both. But interpret newspapers from your Bible."[3] When a racial tragedy occurs in our country—and we know, sadly, many more are coming—our response as race-wise families must be to engage the news through the lens of Scripture.

Gospel-rooted news literacy isn't tied to a political party. As pastor

Joe Carter wrote, "Whether we are getting our news from Fox News or NPR, the fact is the map drawn by the news industry is not likely to match the map of reality produced by its Creator."[4] Carter also said,

> Everything we do should be focused on living in the way God wants us to live. And one of the ways we do that explicitly for the media is to really look at how does this differ from what God is telling me in our Bible. . . . We have a tendency to choose or reject a source of information based on whether we think it's biased. The truth is all sorts of information are biased, since bias is just simply favoring one perspective over another. . . . The truth may be on one end or the other. It may be on the extreme conservative end, it may be on the extreme liberal, and we don't know until we look for the truth.[5]

To have gospel-rooted news literacy means we should continually ask ourselves, What biblical reality should I focus on as I watch the news? How would God want me to respond to this situation? What cultural blind spots do I have? In what ways can the truths of the Bible stretch me right now to see and think differently?

Narrative justice is taking the microphone from the dominant voice and giving other voices—especially those at the margins who are often silenced—the chance to share their stories from their unique perspectives. Ken Wytsma, founder of the Justice Conference, wrote,

> One of the things I have realized and begun to teach is that the message is not only in the content of *what* is taught or presented but also in *who* is bringing it. Indeed, when we address injustices and fight for the oppressed, we can fall into suppressing those we seek to liberate by failing either to shift the power dynamic or to recognize the need for promoting the first-person voice of the oppressed.[6]

In other words, when it comes to the news, we must pursue narrative justice by listening to people of color who have been directly affected by the situation and err on the side of believing their stories.

Slow to Speak and Quick to Listen

What does the Bible have to say about current events? Many parents (and Christians in general for that matter) often wonder whether God's Word is relevant amid the evils facing our world today. Where in Scripture should we turn when a Black or Brown person is shot in the streets or in his or her own home? What does the Bible have to say about immigration, police brutality, systemic racism, missing indigenous women and girls, educational inequity, protests, rioting, and looting? Scripture is full of rich truths about racialized minorities, and God himself models how to care for them especially in the midst of tragedy and loss.

One of the names of God is *El Shama*, meaning "the God who listens or hears." Time and again, when people are hurting, he takes time to listen to their cries. In Genesis 16, Hagar named her son *Ishmael*, meaning "the God who listens," because he heard her desperate call for help in the desert ("for the LORD has heard of your misery," verse 11). Listening is a powerful act. To listen to someone is to validate the truth of his or her story and experience. When God listened to Hagar, he was declaring, "I see you. I believe you."

Similarly, in the New Testament, Jesus listened to the cries of the hurting. In his ministry to the poor, the outcasts of society, women, and others, Jesus placed a high value on listening and validating people's stories. For example, we read in Luke 8:42–48 that Jesus met a woman who had been bleeding for twelve years. After she secretly touched his cloak and was healed, Jesus stopped and asked the woman to publicly share her story: "In the presence of all the people, she told why she had touched him and how she had been instantly healed" (verse 47). It was important to Jesus that people knew this woman's story and believed her. If the woman had simply left after being healed, people may not have accepted the truth of her healing; they may have even accused her of stealing something she didn't deserve. Jesus counteracted any lies that could be told about this woman by calling her "daughter" (verse 48) and publicly declaring that her story mattered. The Jesus who elevates the voices at the margins does far more than listen—he restores those people's dignity as well.

The God who listens, *El Shama*, challenges us parents who are seeking to raise our children with the heart of God to listen to the stories of victimized communities. For example, instead of jumping to talk about grace, forgiveness, and reconciliation with our kids, we need to first encourage ourselves and our kids to do the hard work of hearing a person's or a community's pain and even rage. This listening is what should have happened after the conviction and sentencing of Amber Guyger, a former Dallas police officer who entered twenty-six-year-old Botham Jean's apartment and fatally shot him. Botham's brother, Brandt, responded by saying he forgave Guyger, and then the video of Brandt hugging Guyger went viral.[7] However, many viewers missed the responses of the rest of the family, including these words from Botham's mother, Allison Jean: "Forgiveness for us as Christians is a healing for us, but as my husband said, there are consequences. It does not mean that everything else we have suffered has to go unnoticed."[8] As author and speaker Dorena Williamson argued,

> Listening to the entire Jean family offers us a fuller picture of Christianity. In their words and posture towards Guyger and the criminal justice system, we hear calls for both forgiveness and justice. But if we elevate the words of one family member at the expense of another, we run the risk of distorting the gospel.[9]

Much of the news today on everything from Black Lives Matter to immigrants, border crossings, and anti-Asian racism in this country is steered by the dominant voice. But Scripture challenges us to listen to *all* the voices. We need to turn our attention to the marginalized voices and make the conscious choice to listen to those who have suffered the most pain. We must *listen* and *then respond.* Listening means we respond to a national shooting by saying, "I'm listening. I believe you." It means taking the time to understand the root of people's pain and the ways in which they are asking for care and justice in that moment. We should especially seek to hear the stories of those who are most overlooked in a situation.

Telling your own story is a God-given right. Every person of every cultural background and heritage has the right to talk about his or her struggles and joys. Whether the person is an immigrant, a Black man, a Native American, a Latina, a second-generation Asian American woman, a white person, or someone who is incarcerated, everyone has the right to be heard and believed.

So the next time a racial tragedy headlines the news, our posture as race-wise families should be to listen. The next time a Black or Brown person is killed, the next time immigration is described as "a crisis at the border," or the next time an Asian is the target of racist rhetoric, we must challenge our families to first go to people who represent that community and say, "We must do something! So speak up!"

We must raise children who value people's stories. Whether they are named or unnamed on the nightly news or in a viral video, they are made in the image of God. They each have a story, and their lives have meaning. As you watch the news on television or when your kids are scrolling through news feeds, challenge yourself and your kids to lean into what the victim's family and community are saying. Ask them how people of color might view the situation differently than the news organization reporting the story does. Ask them how a community of color's response is different from the dominant white community's response and why that is.

Only after fully listening *and understanding* can we respond. If we have listened to the voices of hurting people of color—*really* listened—we will challenge ourselves to see the world from their point of view. Current events, including racial tragedies, are always complex, and while there is often room for different opinions, it's important to show love to our neighbors by holding space for and even being led by *their* opinions on an issue. True listening and better understanding lead to holistic responses that align with real community needs and desires.

When we hold the Bible in one hand and the newspaper in the other, our posture as race-wise families will be to listen often and well and to be slow to speak. We will challenge ourselves to hear *all* the voices in a news story and then respond in ways that honor and love those who have been victimized or are struggling.

Living at the Intersection of Love and Wisdom

Responding to current events with both love and wisdom will require intentionality and time. If you want your kids to develop gospel-rooted news literacy, you will need to model it yourself.

Instill in Your Children a Desire to Understand What's Going On in the World

When I (Michelle) was growing up, our family watched thirty minutes of the nightly news together before dinner. It was a routine that we followed Monday through Friday and was something that we looked forward to doing together. What we watched often became the center of our dinnertime conversations or part of subsequent car-ride chats. This might be different from one family to the next, but consider what consistent engagement with the news could look like for you and your kids. Find a rhythm and stick with it. The more your family listens to or watches the news together, the more opportunities will open up for questions and learning.

If your kids have daily screen time, encourage them to spend some of that time learning about the news of the day. Help them develop an interest in what's happening all around the globe. If your child seems particularly interested in a topic, encourage him to research it instead of answering all his questions yourself. Then follow up to learn what he has found.

Take Time to Explain Terms and Larger Contexts

We need to give our children the words and insight to face the ongoing racial dynamics in our country. For example, what happened to George Floyd in 2020 fits into a larger conversation about racial profiling and police brutality. Never assume that your kids understand terms, ideas, and events. Instead, take time to explain things and give definitions. Start educating yourself on issues such as racialized zoning laws and the history of police brutality. Then share what you are learning with your children. (See appendix 5 for suggested resources.)

Moreover, use clear, precise language. Don't say, "People are upset because some groups treat other groups unfairly." Instead, say, "This is about the way that white people treat Black people unfairly."[10] Kenya Hameed, clinical neuropsychologist at the Child Mind Institute, argued that "if you expect children to read between the lines, they can miss the message."[11] If you don't know how to explain something yourself, take time to do the research and learn together. Watch documentaries together. Read books together. It is good and healthy to sometimes tell your children, "I don't know much about this." Your example invites them to hold a similar posture of learning and humility. It also encourages you to learn more as a family, and it can be incredibly special to journey together on a road of racial awareness and sensitivity.

Encourage Your Children's Critical Thinking

Certainly ask your children what they think rather than telling them what to think. But even more than that, instill in them a critical eye that especially notices conspiracies and blanket statements. They should always ask themselves, *How could I be wrong about this?* and *Could I be misleading others?*

For example, many Christians are quick to respond to the death of a Black man at the hands of a white police officer by saying something like "But what about Black-on-Black crime?" However, it's a false equivalence to compare bad policing (or whatever your topic) to Black-on-Black crime. Both are real problems; the latter is a result of the oppression of an entire people group (plus proximity). Hurt people hurt people. There is no reason for Christian families to bring up the crime problem and thereby force people to choose a national agenda item over a minority's lived experiences. Instead of encouraging us to redirect the conversation to Black-on-Black crime or question whether race had anything to do with a killing, God's Word challenges us to open our hearts, stare deadly policing head-on, and embrace a victim's story.

It is particularly important to apply this kind of critical reasoning to larger conversations and ideas about race, especially in light of recent debates over critical race theory (CRT). In 2020, the Council of Seminary Presidents of the Southern Baptist Convention released a statement saying that "Critical Race Theory, Intersectionality and any version of Critical Theory

> **Don't come ready to reject and dismiss. Instead, challenge your family to come as students and see what God might teach you.**

is incompatible with the Baptist Faith & Message."[12] Some SBC pastors have even called for the excommunication of those who promote CRT, arguing that it is "godless" and "Marxist."[13] Black and Brown pastors have left their denomination over the handling of the race conversation.[14] Instead of wholesale denouncing something like critical race theory and telling your children that believing in this idea makes them heretics, spend time studying the topic. Don't base your ideas as a family on just one preacher or a single thought leader. If you're going to develop an opinion on the subject, then you need to first read the work of critical race theorists and thoughtfully engage with a wide spectrum of articles and podcasts by Christians, *especially* Christians of color. If you as a family want to engage in metaconversations about race—perhaps a discussion of CRT, for instance—you and your children should know how to define this idea in its original context and then, at the very least, consider how it might dovetail with a biblical worldview. All truth is God's truth, after all. Don't come ready to reject and dismiss. Instead, challenge your family to come as students and see what God might teach you.

Consider What the Bible Has to Say About the Headlines of the Day

Talk through racial issues with your kids and help them understand current events after looking at those events through a biblical lens. The goal is for our children to engage with the news and come to biblical, gospel-rooted conclusions.

For example, I (Michelle) had been taught as a young child that stealing was wrong. It is, after all, one of the Ten Commandments: "You shall not steal" (Exodus 20:15). Naturally, the first time I witnessed rioting, looting, vandalism, and the destruction of property on a national scale, I assumed that these actions could be viewed only as egregious sins. However, after the rioting and looting that occurred in the wake of George Floyd's death, I read an article by author Patricia Raybon that radically challenged my perspective. Raybon wrote,

[My heart] pulls toward the young people risking arrest and a jail record to pilfer bed sheets and a cart of frozen food. . . .

How will people of faith decide in these matters? Fight for justice? Show the Savior's love? Learn to do both?

I don't have a clear-cut answer. But in times like these, may God help us to arise on His side.[15]

The Bible holds many such paradoxes. There usually is no simple solution to a racial problem. We shouldn't look to the Bible for a quick fix. Rather, each time we are confronted with another tragedy in the news, what we should long for most of all—for ourselves and for our children—is a desire to turn to the Bible and let God guide our hearts, minds, and actions no matter how difficult that research may be or how much God will stretch us.

Practices to Respond to Current Events as a Race-Wise Family

So often critical thinking is caught, not taught. Our kids can learn news literacy not only from hearing what we explain to them but also from observing us. Show them that you yourself are interested in finding reliable news and information. The more we as parents grow in our ability to slow down, assess situations, and pray about the world around us, the more our kids will too. As race-wise families, we can raise our children to have gospel-rooted news literacy. Here are some practices to help you develop this posture together:

1. Equip your kids to identify reliable news stories. When watching the news or reading an article, find the sources cited in the story. "A reliable news story will provide sources for their information and quote people on different sides of an issue," explained Robin Terry Brown, author of *Breaking the News: What's Real, What's Not, and Why the Difference Matters.*[16]

2. When watching the news together, take a few moments to pause the television and reflect on both the text and the images on screen. Ask your children, "What do you see?" and "What message do the words and images convey?" Questions like these equip our children to think about the nuances and complexities of any given issue.

3. Teach your children to stop and think before they click on a news story. "Studies have found that people are much more likely to click on a headline or share a post if it makes them feel happy, angry or excited. And young people are among the most likely to read clickbait," Terry Brown said.[17] Kids need to stop and assess a headline before clicking on it. They should ask themselves, "What kind of emotions is this headline trying to evoke in me?" and "How can I stay calm and not emotionally react to the information I read?" If a child feels that the headline itself is too emotionally volatile, encourage them to come back to the article later or perhaps read a different article instead.

4. As a major local or national racial incident unfolds, regularly check in with your kids and ask them how they're feeling. You can ask questions such as, "How did that news clip make you feel?" and "What emotions are you processing after reading that Instagram post?" Make space for your children to verbally process their emotions. Fight the urge to "fix" their emotions and instead offer responses such as "It's okay to feel frustrated right now. I feel frustrated too" or "I understand that you're sad (or angry or confused). Sometimes the news makes me feel that way too."

5. Offer the following prayer either in your own devotional time or with your family:

God Who Is Sovereign Lord over All,

When the world appears to be falling apart all around us,
bringing a constant stream of tragedy and injustice into our lives
through what we see and hear in the media, help us remember that
nothing happens without your knowledge and attention. Help us
lean into the truths expressed in your Word—that you never sleep
and that you are constantly working for justice and righteousness
even when the path to your purposes is unclear to us. Help us be
race-wise families who are quick to listen and pray and slow to
speak. Give us the discipline to hear all the voices in a news story
and to respond in ways that honor and love those who have been
victimized or who are struggling. Guide us to respond in ways
that don't serve the purposes of the Evil One but promote
goodness, truth, and beauty. We humbly ask that you would
be Lord of our news feeds and our social media engagements
and that nothing we do would detract from your good work
in the world around us.

Amen.

Addressing Privilege

"I DON'T THINK IT'S FAIR for you to always talk about the fact that you have brown skin."

I (Michelle) was in the middle of a conversation with an Anglo-American friend when this comment dropped. In fact, it came right after I shared a painful memory of being body-shamed in high school. I told her how kids in my class had loudly made jokes about my brown skin and hair while pointing at me and laughing. But my friend was skeptical. Not that she didn't think racial profiling existed. Rather, she was frustrated because she felt that Black and Brown people were the only ones allowed to share stories of pain.

She went on to say, "I used to be heavy in high school, and everyone made fun of me for my weight. I was judged by the way I looked and didn't have any friends either."

I nodded and listened. This wasn't the first time I had been in a conversation like this, and it was clear to me that my friend was wrestling with more than just the story I had shared. She took a big breath and concluded, "That's why I don't think you should make a big deal about the fact that you have brown skin.

> **Dismantling our own privilege is part of how we pursue equity in the way God intends.**

People make fun of you for your skin color. People make fun of me for my weight. We both have our struggles, and they're equal."

Conversations like this are tricky to navigate, largely because they are rooted in real experiences of pain and even trauma. We all have been wounded in different ways, and sometimes it's hard to hear about someone else's struggle when you're still hurting. I wanted to share more about why our experiences were different, but it was important for me to do so without making my friend feel like I was delegitimizing the pain she had endured. So, after affirming her and hearing more of her story, I carefully proceeded, saying, "Yes, you're right. Each of us can be shamed in different ways. It was wrong that people shamed you for your weight in high school. It was also wrong that you experienced disadvantages in high school as a result. But it's important to not treat every struggle as the same. That would be like seeing every form of cancer as the same. If we do that, we'll think we can treat each cancer the same way, which would be disastrous. Body-shaming is one kind of disease that requires a specific form of care. Racial prejudice and racist actions against a person because of the color of their skin is a wholly different kind of disease and requires a completely different treatment and cure."

I went on to say, "You weren't shamed for the color of your skin, which meant that your white skin wasn't a factor in any of the disadvantages you experienced in high school. In that sense, you had a privilege as a student that I didn't. My reality as the lone brown-skinned girl in an all-white high school meant I experienced a number of disadvantages that you didn't. The cards weren't stacked against us equally."

My friend didn't initially agree with me. When you've felt abnormal in some way and experienced hurt and shame as a result, it's hard to be told that you could still be more privileged than others are. It's hard to hear that, despite your hardships, you have advantages over others.

This chapter maps out how we must consider where we benefit most, where we hold power over others, and how we can dismantle our own privilege and put the interests of others above our own. Perhaps contrary to popular belief, the goal of deconstructing privilege isn't to achieve equality. Rather, dismantling our own privilege is part of how we pursue equity in the way God intends. We have to flip the script, and this will actually feel very unequal. God lifts up the weak and disempowered, and he gives greater honor to those on the margins. The goal of dismantling our power and privilege is to embrace new, sacrificial ways of living because that is what Jesus chose to do for us (Philippians 2:6–8).

Defining Terms

We understand how complicated and emotionally charged these terms are. But it's important to understand how the general population is using this language so we can construct a biblical framework for processing and using the language ourselves.

Privilege is, at its core, an advantage or set of advantages, and it is something that we all can have, albeit in different ways and different degrees. Privilege can exist because of our race, gender, class, physical abilities, mental abilities, body type, and more. Whenever our society values a particular quality more than others, a form of privilege exists. Though these areas of privilege may not completely define who we are as persons, we can't ignore how certain advantages shape our experiences in unique ways.

White privilege, a term popularized by activist and scholar Peggy McIntosh,[1] refers to the fact that people with white skin often experience certain advantages in life over people with black and brown skin. Having white privilege is like wearing a safety badge as you go through your day. It protects you from being judged, profiled, or discriminated against based on the color of your skin. In contrast, many people of color—Black people in particular—have the police called on them simply for doing regular activities. Whether they are waiting for a friend at Starbucks, barbecuing at a park, working out at the gym, or asking for directions, people of color are often put in danger because they are deemed suspicious or dangerous.[2] In contrast, many white people don't have to worry when approached by a cop.

White privilege is tethered to the long, complicated history of **racialization**, a system of values that says one group of people is superior to all others because of the color of their skin. The system of white superiority has served as the foundation for the oppression and subjugation of non-white people both in the history of the United States and around the world. Wherever white people have waged wars and conquered territories, racism has followed. As Cory Collins wrote in an article on white privilege, "Colonialism, slavery, Jim Crow laws, and mass incarceration came out of the belief that white people should enjoy a certain standard of living built on the backs of lesser peoples." Collins later wrote, "White privilege is both a legacy and a cause of racism."[3] White privilege continues to reinforce systemic racism today.

White supremacy is the preferential treatment of white people supported by the belief that the lives and experiences of white people have more value than those of Black and Brown people. These beliefs can be traced far back into the history of our nation, and they were even written into our founding documents. As Mark Charles and Soong-Chan Rah pointed out in their book *Unsettling Truths*, both the Declaration of Independence and the Constitution clearly prioritize white, land-owning men while also referring to indigenous peoples as "merciless Indian Savages"[4] and Black slaves as three-fifths of a person.[5] Charles and Rah wrote,

The myth of Anglo-Saxon superiority girds the imagination that elevates the white body, mind, language, and culture. The Declaration of Independence . . . is rooted in the assumption of the exceptional rational capacity of the ethnically pure, white European—now American.[6]

Our nation must contend with the reality that its founding beliefs demean people who, though made in God's image, were deemed less than those people of European descent who believed themselves to be superior. Ultimately, these foundational beliefs paved the way for those who are white to be considered more valuable. In other words, for white supremacy.

White supremacy is an important idea for Christians to understand. A recent Barna study called *Beyond Diversity*, undertaken in partnership with the Racial Justice and Unity Center and sociologist Michael Emerson, found that "only two in five white practicing Christians (38%) believe the U.S. has a race problem," in contrast to 78 percent of Black practicing Christians. Similarly, "three-quarters of Black practicing Christians (75%) at least somewhat agree that the U.S. has a history of oppressing minorities, while white practicing Christians are less likely to do so (42%)."[7] To put it simply, white and non-white Christians hold vastly polarized views on issues of race and its impact on minorities in this country. Sadly, as long as white Christians don't believe in the historical realities of white supremacy, the white church—and, by extension, white Christian families—will neglect a fundamental part of their Christian witness.

Disprivilege, by contrast, is a set of disadvantages that make it harder for a person to succeed. One of these disadvantages is colorism, the reality that people with darker skin colors are treated as inferior, looked at more suspiciously by the police, and are less likely to be considered for jobs, leadership positions, and more. Every community ascribes value to skin color in different ways and can be guilty of perpetuating colorism.[8]

Colorism exists not only between dominant and subdominant cultures such as white and Black but also between African American, Asian American, Latino American, and Native American communities. Thus, as people of color, we, too, must be conscious of whether we are discriminating against another person of color because of his or her skin color.

Disprivileges can diminish a person's quality of life; they can also endanger it. In East Austin where I (Michelle) live, white students have brought drugs to high school and were given nothing more than a disciplinary warning. I've had conversations with the parents of these students, and the parents themselves expressed shock at how lenient the administration was to their children. At the same time, Black students I know personally who have done the same thing were arrested on-site and placed in juvenile detention. I've also witnessed the police body-slam a student to the ground and handcuff them in front of their peers, which is incredibly shaming to the student. Research has shown that "school administrators treat black students differently than their white counterparts."[9] The US Department of Education's Civil Rights Data Collection has shown that Black students are more likely to receive school suspensions than white students.[10] Research has also shown that students who have been suspended from school often fall behind in key metrics such as reading skills. As Brett Arends noted, researchers said, "The more students fall behind, the less likely they are to graduate from high school or enter college and the more likely they are to become incarcerated. This dangerous cycle is called the school-to-prison pipeline."[11] When disprivileges are stacked one on top of another, they can negatively affect the whole course of a person's life.

A Biblical Approach to Privilege

Our children need to understand their own privilege. More than that, we have to teach them that giving up our privileges for

> **Our children need to understand their own privilege. More than that, we have to teach them that giving up our privileges for the sake of others is at the very core of our Christian faith.**

the sake of others is at the very core of our Christian faith. When it comes to the issue of privilege, the posture of a race-wise family should be one of humility, stewardship, and generosity. We must ask God to open our hearts and our hands to joyfully share what we have with those who have less. We give not out of shame or guilt but out of the abundance of the heart and because of our commitment to the way of Christ.

The posture of open hands and hearts is at the core of biblical stewardship. The parable of the talents in Matthew 25:14–30 teaches us that we as believers are called to utilize and manage "all resources God provides for the glory of God and the betterment of His creation."[12] The Bible says that "every good and perfect gift is from above, coming down from the Father" (James 1:17). God has given each of us privileges, which can include but are not limited to our family, our job, our health, our athletic abilities, our friends, our home, certain freedoms in this country, and other basic provisions. Both of us are intentional about spending time with our families in thankfulness for God's good gifts. We thank God at mealtimes and throughout our day for the good things he has given us. Yet we, as individuals and as families, are mindful that God also calls us to use our privileges to serve and care for others. We must be willing to share what we have so that those with less can flourish.

When we're talking about stewardship and privilege, it's important to remember the self-emptying love of Jesus. He gave up his rights and privileges to come to earth, walk among humans, and save us from our sins. In Mark 8:34–35, Jesus said, "Whoever wants to be my disciple must deny themselves and take up their cross and follow me. For whoever wants to save their life will lose it, but whoever loses their life for me and for the gospel will save it." And Philippians 2:7–8 says that Jesus

> emptied himself,
>> taking the form of a slave,
>> being born in human likeness.
> And being found in human form,
>> he humbled himself
>> and became obedient to the point of death—
>> even death on a cross. (NRSV)

Jesus chose to lose (i.e., to die for our sins) so that we could win. He sacrificed his own privileges and became our equal in order to heal and save us. When we follow the model of Jesus's self-sacrifice, we give up our rights and advantages out of love for God and love for our neighbors.

People often think that the conversation on privilege and related topics such as reparations—broadly defined by pastors Duke Kwon and Gregory Thompson as "the deliberate repair of White supremacy's cultural theft through restitution (returning what one wrongfully took) and restoration (restoring the wronged to wholeness)"[13]—boils down to money. That logic, unfortunately, leads people to think that conversations on reparations are simply about trying to take their financial assets. However, biblically speaking, reparations is far more complex. Again, as Kwon and Thompson argued, reparations involves repairing and restoring what has been stolen, specifically, truth, power, and wealth. If we want to lay down our rights the way Jesus did, we must be willing to rethink our perspective on the past (i.e., our nation's history), on who gets to lead the conversations about race, and on how we bear each other's social, financial, and racial burdens. That subject matter may feel overwhelming for us adults to navigate, let alone try to explain to our children. So we're going to start with a baby step. If we want to repair and restore our brothers and sisters who have been marginalized because of white privilege, a good first step is considering how much we are willing to share with others.

Laying down our privileges and rights for others means we embrace a posture of sharing. For example, how often do you encourage your children to share? Have you ever had conversations with them about giving away something they have? In Indian culture, it's common to give someone—even a complete stranger—the coat off your back. Growing up, I (Michelle) remember many times when my mother would hand over her earrings or bracelet to someone simply because that person complimented her. This posture of generosity is essential to the sacrificial life we as followers of Jesus are supposed to lead. We give what we have—whether it's a toy, our money, that unused bedroom in our home, our car, our time, our knowledge, our skills, or our network connections—and we give abundantly out of the joy and gratitude in our hearts.

Both of our families make it a habit to pack water bottles and bagged snacks whenever we go for a drive. That way, if we happen to see someone experiencing homelessness, we can roll down our window and offer him or her food and drink. These moments become an opportunity for us to share what we have and thereby show the sacrificial love of Jesus. When we give food and drink or sometimes money to someone experiencing homelessness, I (Michelle) make sure to remind my children that God loves that man or woman, and so should we. I then reiterate to them that the reason we give what we can to those in need is that God has blessed us with money, food, and drink that others don't have, and sharing is how we steward what has been given to us.

Admittedly, sharing can be hard. We don't always understand why other people say they need certain things, and we can be hesitant to give when a request feels more like a disgruntled person's demand. If you ever feel that way in conversations about privilege, remind yourself, *This person doesn't experience the world the way I do. She doesn't have the same benefits that I do. How might God be calling me to help right now?*

The reality is, it *is* hard to understand why people are asking for things to be different. Whether it's a demand for wheelchair accessibility, sign language and closed captions for videos, or racial equity, we need a robust imagination to see the world through other people's eyes and consider how different their lives are from our own. As we navigate these difficult conversations, we should pray for the Spirit to help us empathize, care, and understand the real problems being expressed and how we can respond with generous, open hearts.

More than that, we and our children need to have eyes to see that some of our rights and privileges were acquired *because* other people weren't allowed to flourish. In Luke's gospel, Zacchaeus confronted his own privilege. At first, we see that he benefited from the economic system as a tax collector. Luke 19 says that Zacchaeus was "a chief tax collector" (verse 2, NRSV). Tax collectors are interesting characters in the Bible. Typically, they were Jewish people who extorted their fellow Jews on behalf of the Roman Empire. Tax collectors would often charge people more than was due so that they could pocket some of the money. As a result, they unfairly benefited from their power over others.

We know from the text that Zacchaeus was rich (verse 2). In the story, Jesus went to his house, and Zacchaeus responded by saying, "Look, half of my possessions, Lord, I will give to the poor; and if I have defrauded anyone of anything, I will pay back four times as much" (verse 8, NRSV). Then Jesus said, "Today salvation has come to this house, because he too is a son of Abraham. For the Son of Man came to seek out and to save the lost" (verses 9–10, NRSV). As attorney Anna Feingold argued, "Although the legal system permitted the benefit Zacchaeus accrued, he chooses to treat that benefit as an illicit act causing criminal harm, and to provide restitution accordingly. The system did not treat the benefit to Zacchaeus as theft. But he holds himself to a higher standard than the worldly system in which he operates."[14]

It's no easy task to consider as a family whether some of your rights and privileges are hurting others. We also don't need to look at every good gift in our lives as if we're criminals who stole it. Nevertheless, the possible negative impact of our good gifts on others is an important aspect of the conversation on stewardship and privilege that shouldn't be ignored. We must consider whether the comforts we enjoy have come at the expense of someone else, and if they have, that should bother us. Stewarding our resources and privileges should include considering whether we may, in fact, need to give monetary reparations, move houses, or change where our children attend school so that we don't feed into a system that benefits some people over others.

Since making major life decisions can feel daunting, it helps to begin by focusing on tangible privileges like money, toys, and nice clothes before addressing more intangible privileges like skin color or ethnicity. Like in the parable of the talents, if our children can understand how to give generously in small, individual ways, God will cultivate in them the posture of humility, stewardship, and generosity they will need in order to address bigger social and systemic issues in the future.

Three Steps Forward

Now that we're becoming more aware of our privilege as racewise families, what do we do with that insight? And how do we show our children what an appropriate response looks like? Sometimes we will be proactive, but sometimes we will find ourselves on the defensive.

If Someone Says, "Watch Your Privilege," Notice If You Sense Your Defenses Rising

Returning to Luke 19, it's notable that, in the face of questions about privilege, Zacchaeus wasn't defensive. As the crowd grumbled and even openly criticized him, Zacchaeus didn't lash out. He didn't try to explain why he actually deserved the benefits that he had accrued. He didn't try to deflect blame or point out flaws in his accusers. He "stood there" (verse 8, NRSV)—present to the criticism, not trying to escape the discomfort. As parents, we need to model the same.

Like Zacchaeus, we must show our children that we don't fear criticism. Rather than getting angry, we can demonstrate active listening. I (Michelle) argued that point in an article for the Asian American Christian Collaborative (AACC):

> A significant part of deconstructing white privilege is learning to listen and respond instead of leading. Being humble means using your platform to model being a good listener. Putting someone else's interests above your own means asking questions and choosing not to be triggered by the term *white privilege,* or insisting that people of color rewrite the rulebook to make you less uncomfortable.[15]

Moreover, we have to stay focused. We often become defensive when we feel we're being unfairly targeted. We've heard from more than one white person that they feel that conversations about white privilege and white supremacy are instigated by those who just hate white folks. For the most part, this isn't true. But we have to challenge ourselves not to take these conversations personally and make them all about us. Naming white privilege is simply acknowledging evil and oppressive systems in our midst, not about white people being inherently bad.

So let's have the hard conversations. As families, let's commit to listening well, asking good questions, and humbly choosing to do better.

Name and Own Your Privilege

All of us—both parents and kids—need to acknowledge our personal advantages. If we don't, we won't understand our own complicity in the system of privilege. Though it will be hard and at times uncomfortable, we need to examine which doors have been opened for us and why.

For example, as Asian American women, both Helen and I have been underprivileged in many areas of life. Both of us have been shamed for the color of our skin. I (Michelle) have even been refused service at a restaurant because of my brown skin. Helen was explicitly shamed for being Asian in an otherwise all-white sixth-grade classroom and called numerous racial slurs throughout her adolescence and into college. However, we have both experienced advantages too. We are both college educated. Neither of us is disabled. Both of us live in cities and rub shoulders with like-minded people. We are both safely housed, have disposable income, and are relatively light skinned. (Many Indians have darker skin than I do, and dark-skinned Indians are, sadly, often treated both in the US and in India as less beautiful and less qualified for jobs than fair-skinned Indians.) Helen and I have to reckon with our mixed reality of privileges and disprivileges. We have been on this journey to recognize the opportunities withheld from us because of our status as women of color and at the same time to also identify our platforms and power that enable us to use what we have been given for the benefit of those less privileged.

No matter our ethnic and racial heritage, recognizing our own privileges is a necessary step in working toward a more equitable and just future, both inside and outside the home. There are times when we have advantages that others don't and times when we can speak when others won't be heard. More importantly, we can use these advantages to fight systems of oppression.

Leverage Your Privilege for Good

When we confront our own privilege, we'll find opportunities to help others. Awareness leads to action. When we understand our own privilege, we can work toward dismantling the systems of racial oppression that benefit us. We all must want racism and other human hierarchies eradicated. Whether we're part of the dominant or a subdominant culture, we need to identify the privilege in our own lives and communities and be willing to share what we have with others. Jesus calls us to lay down our rights, to humble ourselves, and to love all the unique people around us so that they feel cared for instead of looked down on.

We can begin by thinking through what supportive physical presence looks like. How do we show support to others with our actions and our voices? Sometimes it's as simple as saying something when we see something. We can use our voices whenever we see unjust treatment of a Black and/or Brown person or community. Many of us have voices that carry power, and if we courageously say, "This is wrong," people will listen. Our children should hear us raise our voices regularly so that speaking truth boldly is part of the daily rhythms of our families. We can also show up for local marches and protests. We can attend meetings at our churches or schools where people of color are raising important issues that need to be addressed. Our presence communicates, "I care. This is important." We can also encourage our children to be allies to their classmates and other peers simply by sitting with them at the lunch table or in class or by playing with them at recess.

On a systemic level, we can leverage our platforms, power, and resources to protect people who have been marginalized and oppressed. We can use our voices to make deep shifts in the hiring practices, culture, and philosophy of our organizations and churches. We can also support educational equality for low-income schools; challenge law enforcement and prosecutor misconduct, including

> **Jesus calls us to lay down our rights, to humble ourselves, and to love all the unique people around us so that they feel cared for instead of looked down on.**

issues of police brutality; advocate for pardon or commutation for those incarcerated because of minor misdemeanors; drastically change the criminal legal system; and listen to those who have the best understanding of whether financial reparations can help address systemic issues in our neighborhoods.[16] In all these efforts, we should faithfully listen to God's voice and to the voices of those on the margins before we take action.

Practices to Cultivate Humility, Stewardship, and Generosity as a Race-Wise Family

Talk to your children early and often about privilege and racial injustice. Help them see and understand privilege in their own lives and in the world around them. Remember, when we seek to dismantle our own power and privilege, we live more like Jesus, who modeled a life of humility, stewardship, and generosity. Here are several ways we can cultivate this posture in our own homes:

1. Read books and other resources on privilege. We recommend the short comic "Race Matters: A Story About White Privilege"[17] as a starting point along with *Not My Idea: A Book About Whiteness* by Anastasia Higginbotham and *Race Cars: A Children's Book About White Privilege* by Jenny Devenny. Give your kids space to process the pictures and big ideas, and follow up with questions such as "Why did the white man and the Black man have such different experiences?" Also, make time for a family reading of the 1989 article "White Privilege: Unpacking the Invisible Knapsack" by Peggy McIntosh and *The Hate U Give* by Angie Thomas for tween-age children and above.

2. Introduce your high schoolers to illustrations of privilege on social media. For example, in dancer Allison Holker's viral TikTok, she and her husband, who is Black,

take Big Mamma's "Check Your Privilege" challenge, which includes instructions like "Put a finger down if you have been stopped or detained by police for no valid reason" and "Put a finger down if you have been bullied solely because of your race."[18] Then ask your kids to hold up their fingers and take the test as well. You and your kids can also watch Cut's "Black Parents Explain How to Deal with the Police" to illustrate this point.[19]

3. Find opportunities in everyday life to point to examples of white privilege. If a news story comes on about police violence against Black Americans, talk about documented examples of white people being treated differently by law enforcement. Show your children (perhaps age ten and above) a picture of armed white protesters and have a conversation.

4. Make it your goal that by the time your kids are in high school, they will know about the explicit and implicit racial biases that affect people's access to occupational and educational opportunities. Challenge your teens to come up with examples from their own lives—from school, work, and sports. Talk to them about privilege and, by extension, racism so they can both better identify issues and become interested in fighting for positive change.

5. Make time at the dinner table or on family evenings to regularly talk about how you can dismantle privilege. Remind your family that privilege is simply any advantage, benefit, or right that someone has that others don't. Spend time praying about and discussing both the privileges your family has *and* ways you can use your privilege for good.

6. Offer the following prayer either in your own devotional time or with your family:

God of the Disprivileged,

You lift up the weak and disempowered, and you give greater honor to those on the margins. May we desire to do the same. Give our family wisdom, boldness, and humility as we make conversations about privilege and racial injustice part of our everyday lives. May we and our children see and understand privilege in our own lives and in the world around us, and grant us the courage to give up our privileges for the sake of others. We recognize that dismantling our own power and privilege will be costly, but that is the way of Jesus. We want to be a race-wise family, and this means learning to flip the script and to pursue equity in the way you intend. God, fortify us for this journey.

Amen.

Assessing Our Biases

WHEN MY (HELEN'S) ELDEST SON, Jason, was a tween, he would regularly ask me to describe him, and he would enjoy hearing my assessment—"You are bright, helpful, musically gifted, self-confident, and a social butterfly!"—even if I generally said the same thing every time he asked. There is something reassuring about having your self-assessment confirmed by others and something intriguing about discovering that other people might see you differently than you see yourself. Although we might think we know ourselves best, studies in the field of self-perception show that parts of ourselves are unknown to us. Especially when it comes to matters of race, we might not have a realistic perspective of who we are and what assumptions we are carrying.

You likely already understand that racial issues are real, that racism still exists, and that part of our calling as Christians is to stand against racism in any form. But if you are still fairly new to the journey of becoming race-wise, the reality is that you may have never had to fully address whatever biases undergird your beliefs and lifestyle. This isn't the kind of internal work that happens on its own. Similar to the ways in which our bodies can carry diseases without our knowledge, we are often unaware of the ways in which we are holding on to perspectives that can be damaging to our quests to honor God in the area of racial and ethnic understanding. We might have the desire to become race-wise, but we also have to acknowledge that it's challenging to view ourselves accurately and yield to the true transformation of our mindsets.

Sanctification in any area of our lives is never automatic or easy. The Christian life is a journey of growing in self-awareness and embracing repentance. Spiritual forces are strong within each of us to *not* do the right thing even if we know it's the right thing. In Romans 7:18–19, Paul wrote, "I know that good itself does not dwell in me, that is, in my sinful nature. For I have the desire to do what is good, but I cannot carry it out. For I do not do the good I want to do, but the evil I do not want to do—this I keep on doing." When we are talking about an area as complex and challenging as race, our underlying inclinations combined with our uncertainties and hesitations about this topic often result in inertia, ignorance, and apathy even for the most well-intentioned of Christians.

Defining Terms

In addition to the realities of our sin nature, we are each prone to misunderstandings and prejudices due to any number of factors—geography, demographics, our communities, influences from family and friends, and our media consumption, to name a few. Unpacking those underlying assumptions will take some work.

The phrase **conscious bias** refers to those preferences or prejudices we know we hold about categories of people. These prejudices can be stereotypical in nature, such as believing that all Asians are good at math and science; they can result in actions that are discriminatory, such as favoring those who are white in hiring decisions or even more extreme expressions of racism.

We may be explicit about these biases or we may conceal them, but we ourselves are conscious that they are present.

On the other end of this spectrum is the category of **implicit bias**. The Kirwan Institute for the Study of Race and Ethnicity defines *implicit bias* as "the attitudes or stereotypes that affect our understanding, actions, and decisions in an unconscious manner."[1] These biases can be positive or negative, but we aren't even conscious that we have them. Here are additional points that the institute notes about implicit bias:

- Implicit biases are pervasive. Everyone possesses them, even people with avowed commitments to impartiality, such as judges.
- The implicit associations we hold do not necessarily align with our declared beliefs or even reflect stances we would explicitly endorse.
- We generally tend to hold implicit biases that favor our own in-group, though research has shown that we can still hold implicit biases against our in-group.[2]

The good news is that biases don't have to be permanent. We can educate ourselves and take intentional steps to counter them. Project Implicit, a nonprofit organization led by psychology professors from Harvard University and the University of Virginia, has a growing collection of implicit bias tests that we can take as a self-check.[3] These can be helpful tools to unpack preferences we may be carrying for or against other racial and ethnic groups. None of us are unmarred by the effects of our sin nature, and biases are a part of that nature. Taking assessments such as these can make us more aware of the places where we fall short of valuing God's image in each human being he created.

In this chapter, we will also introduce you to our own Multi-ethnicity Quotient, a simple tool that we have created to help you better understand where your own biases and assumptions come from and what areas in your life might require some intentional action in order for you to become race-wise. As the apostle James exhorted us, "My brothers and sisters, believers in our glorious Lord Jesus Christ must not show favoritism" (James 2:1). Change may not be easy or fast, but as we come before God with humility, asking for his transforming Spirit to continue to work within us, we can trust that he will make us more like Christ, who loves and died for all people without prejudice.

When We Read the Bible with Bias

The first step in assessing our biases is to consider our interpretation of Scripture, as E. Randolph Richards and Brandon J. O'Brien addressed in their book *Misreading Scripture with Western Eyes:*

> Becoming aware of our cultural assumptions and how they influence our reading of Scripture are important first steps . . . toward a faithful reading and application of the Bible. . . .
>
> If our cultural blind spots keep us from *reading* the Bible correctly, then they can also keep us from *applying* the Bible correctly.[4]

We each bring our own experiences and assumptions whenever we come to God's Word.

It's helpful to supplement our own understanding of Scripture with the perspectives of those who are different from us. Many Bible commentaries on the market are written by those from a European American background; while those resources are valuable in and of themselves, they won't be able to reflect the full range of perspectives and experiences that can help us see God through lenses that aren't our own.

Take, for example, the story of Joseph and his sons in Genesis 48, after Joseph had been reconciled to his family in an extraordinary fashion. His father, Jacob, was about to bless Joseph's sons who, as theologian and New Testament professor

Esau McCaulley noted, were half-Jewish, half-Egyptian. Yet Jacob claimed Ephraim and Manasseh as his own, thereby filling out what would become the twelve tribes of Israel in a multiethnic fashion. McCaulley wrote,

> Jacob sees the *Brown flesh and African origin of these boys* as the beginning of God's fulfillment of his promise to make Jacob a community of different nations and ethnicities, and *for that reason he claims these two boys as his own.* . . . Egypt and Africa are not *outside* of God's people; African blood flows *into* Israel from the beginning as a fulfillment of the promise made to Abraham, Isaac, and Jacob.[5]

This story is familiar to many Christians, yet those of us who aren't of African or African American descent may have missed this key point that establishes the multiethnic nature of the Abrahamic covenant. From the outset, God has intended for his people to be diverse, and we see evidence of this all the way back in Genesis. With our limited perspectives and our unconscious biases, none of us understand the fullness of God. But the more we come to grips with those limits, the more open we become to shoring up our own areas of deficient knowledge with the perspectives of those who can help us see God more clearly.

What to Know Before You Face Yourself

Assessing our biases is one of the hardest postures to embrace as a race-wise family because it involves facing truths about yourself that you may never have known existed. We, as parents, have to do this work first. However, as you are learning and growing in this area, we encourage you to share any epiphanies you might experience with your spouse and your children. Modeling this part of your journey will encourage your whole family in their journey to becoming race-wise. Mentally prepare for this process by reminding yourself that you do have biases—we all do—but that the grace of God covers and makes up for all our shortcomings. God's love means not only that he accepts us for who we are but also that he loves us too much to let us stay the same. So embrace any new insights, as challenging as that task may be, and allow those moments to lead you to deeper understanding and change.

When I (Helen) was working as a cashier at my mom's sandwich shop one summer, I would regularly serve a Black woman who bought the same breakfast every day. My mom's frugality meant that we would give out bags only to customers who asked instead of automatically offering them. Most of our customers would just dash out the door with their food or candy bar in hand. But each time this woman checked out, she asked for a bag with a sour expression and a disdainful tone. Frustrated by her attitude, I made assumptions about her motivations and beliefs: *She must not like Asian people.* So—although I knew she would ask for a bag each time she came—instead of offering one to her, I would wait until she asked.

But as this continued day after day, I felt the Holy Spirit nudging me: *Talk with her. Don't assume you understand.* So the next time she asked for a bag for her food, I did just that. I said, "I'm sorry that I wait for you to ask for a bag each time, but my mom only wants me to offer them to customers who ask for them. Would you like me to just give you one whenever you check out?"

She looked me squarely in the eye and said, "I ask for a bag each time because I was taught that if I don't, someone will assume that I have stolen what I have bought. The bag protects me from being unfairly accused of being a thief."

I will never forget the shame I felt in that moment as all my own biases were revealed; I had assumed something that was so completely off base and a reflection of my own sinful nature. After I thanked her for sharing, I silently offered gratitude to

God for giving me a window into what was really happening in these interactions, and I asked him to forgive me for acting on my false assumptions. From that day forward, I always bagged her food without her asking. She, in turn, lost her edge, and over time her sour face gradually relaxed into an expression of peace—if not a full smile—when she entered.

Just a smidgen of deeper understanding can transform our interactions with people around us, especially those who are different from us. As we open ourselves to the Spirit's leading and submit ourselves to learning about even the deepest, darkest biases we might have, God does his soul work to repair the breaches in us, which is what is needed in order for us to repair the breaches in one another.

Last, commit to persevering in this process because this is a journey that won't end until God completes his work in you, which we know he will (Philippians 1:6). In his book *Tempered Resilience*, Tod Bolsinger explained that when we are in the crucible of hardships, when everything feels difficult and we feel most off balance and inept, our character is being forged and ultimately strengthened as we stay committed to the work that we are doing and that God is doing in us.[6]

Awareness as the Antidote

There is no better way to address your biases than to become aware of them and of what lifestyle choices and attitudes may be increasing or maintaining these biases. Although there are many possible areas of bias in our lives, for the purpose of this book, we are focusing on biases of a cultural, ethnic, or racial nature. To reduce or eradicate these biases, we must increase our multiethnic awareness and analyze the tendencies and beliefs that we have sometimes without even realizing it.

We suggest that you take a closer look at these five Cs of multiethnic awareness, which you can analyze more fully through our Multiethnicity Quotient assessment. As you read through these sections, do a mental assessment of where you stand and where you could use more intentional effort to counter potential areas of bias.

Community

One way to assess your multiethnic awareness is to look at your personal relationships. As you get to know others who are different from you and come to understand their journeys, trials, and experiences better, changes will happen in you that you might not have expected.

I (Helen) had a good friend in college who grew up in an entirely white neighborhood and school. When we met, Rose hadn't ever had any friends of color. But the college Christian fellowship group was quite diverse, and suddenly Rose found herself becoming close friends with numerous people of color, including several Korean Americans. A whole new world opened up for her as she began to understand the differences in the way she and her friends of color had grown up. She developed a deep affection for Korean culture in particular, which led her to bravely try new foods and even devote a portion of her college studies to learning the Korean language. As she grew to love her Christian brothers and sisters of all ethnic backgrounds, she gained great appreciation for their cultural nuances and relational styles. And it all started in the context of relationships.

The challenge for most of us is that we tend to gravitate toward those who are most like us ethnically, socioeconomically, generationally, etc. And this also applies to our kids. A study by Duke University sociologist James Moody found that "the more diverse the school, the more the kids self-segregate by race and ethnicity within the school, and thus the likelihood that any two kids of different races have a friendship goes down."[7] Our sin nature craves comfort, ease, and familiarity. So when it comes to connecting with other people, we often have to be prodded by the Spirit to build relationships with those who are different from us. When Jesus answered the Jewish law expert's question "Who is my neighbor?" (Luke 10:29), note that he chose to depict the Samaritan as the good neighbor—and most of the Jewish listeners would have automatically viewed the Samaritan negatively. Our relationships, whether personal, professional, or casual, are a large indicator of how comfortable we are with multiethnicity, and changes in this area will spill over into other areas of our lives.

So, if you find yourself in largely monoethnic situations, start asking the Lord to bring people into your life from a variety of backgrounds to help you broaden your relational horizons. Open your eyes to see whom you might have either knowingly or unintentionally avoided. If you truly want to follow the Lord's leading in this area, you don't have to worry about tokenism—befriending people merely because they help you meet some kind of internal diversity quota—and you can rest assured that God will open relational doors as you increase your readiness for those new connections.

Consumerism

"You are what you eat," we often tell our children in order to help them make good nutritional choices that will strengthen their bodies. But the same concept is true of everything we consume: what we read, watch, and listen to has a cumulative effect, negative or positive, on our minds, hearts, and souls. Often we are influenced by recommendations from people we trust. (Ask anyone in the book industry what the most effective way of marketing books is, and that person will tell you that word of mouth has more impact than any multimillion-dollar ad campaign ever could.) So, circling back to community, the more multiethnic your personal and professional networks are, the more likely you will be to see and hear recommendations that reflect multiethnic values.

If you sense that you're weak in the area of multiethnic community and you don't want to lag behind in this area of consumerism as well, you will need to take initiative. Start by looking at your favorite areas of popular culture. What kinds of shows do you gravitate to, and what kinds of people do they feature? What kinds of books do you most appreciate and most frequently read? What styles of music do you listen to most often? Asking these kinds of questions helps you assess your own lifestyle choices, which you may have never thought about before. If you notice that you don't typically watch television shows or movies with diverse casts, for example, that knowledge alone will begin to raise your self-awareness and motivate you to intentionally choose media that will expand your multiethnic horizons.

Half the battle is in the area of noticing one's own tendencies and preferences. Most people aren't even aware that they have fallen into comfortable patterns that keep them from experiencing a more multiethnic life. Our own cultural lenses keep us from being able to see that, from the beginning, God's intention was for us to create multiethnic households, to live multiethnic lives, and thereby to reflect his love to a broken and divided world. Taking the time to see how our preferences have translated into what information we consume is a key step toward a more multiethnic life.

Christian Living

Many Christians have heard the famous statement by Martin Luther King Jr. that eleven o'clock on Sunday morning is the most segregated time in the US.[8] Yet knowing that reality hasn't significantly changed the landscape of the church in the past few decades. Data from 2019 indicated that in 23 percent of evangelical churches in the US, at least 20 percent of their members represent diverse people groups. While this shows progress since 1998—when only 7 percent of evangelical churches could say the same[9]—the US has a long way to go until the majority of American Christians experience a multiethnic worship setting. (And for some Americans, such as recent immigrants for whom English isn't a primary language, a monocultural context is the preferred way for them to meet and know God.)

Given the reality that most American Christians still worship in largely white or monoethnic settings, what can people of faith do to create a more multiethnic Christian life, aside from seeking out churches where they are in the cultural minority? In the church context, an individual Christian can help bring about changes by raising questions about worship styles, suggesting practices of lament after instances of racial injustice occur, or proposing book studies for small groups and adult Sunday school classes that can help increase multiethnic understanding. It's one thing for people of color to make these types of suggestions; when those who are from the dominant culture do so, it demonstrates that the congregation cares about the entirety of the body of Christ and not just about those in the majority.

As you begin to notice who is given the opportunity to preach and teach, what kinds of books you study together as a church, and whether the concerns of those people on the margins are reflected in times of prayer and in church life, you can share your growing awareness with leaders. You might even volunteer to lead a class, discussion, or initiative and be a part of your congregation's movement forward. Moving a church in the direction of multiethnicity isn't a fast or easy process, but without congregants raising these issues and following through with action, no congregation can make progress in this area. Progress can come, however, with focused effort based on the convictions of those in positions of authority and power. And you may be just the person called to catalyze the growth process at your church.

Cross-Cultural Competency

How often does your family have the chance to experience a cultural context that isn't your own? This can happen easily: try another cultural cuisine, study a language aside from English, or travel outside the United States if you're able. These efforts help families understand how big the world is and, by extension, how varied the people are whom God in his infinite wisdom created.

By virtue of being married to a Canadian, I (Helen) have had the unique opportunity to learn how non-Americans perceive the US. It has been so helpful for me and my children to understand that Americans suffer from an overly strong sense of exceptionalism. This inflated sense of national self is reflected in everything from political rhetoric that never fails to affirm the greatness of the United States (heard from both sides of the political aisle) to the ways in which our nation relates to other countries (often with a protectionist rather than a generous posture). And this mentality runs counter to a multiethnic perspective that honors and appreciates the blessings that come from "every nation, tribe, people and language" God has created (Revelation 7:9).

It might not be easy to take a trip to the other side of the world, but perhaps once a month your family could take a virtual trip to another country by researching a different culture, watching shows or videos that educate you about that people group, and making food from that culture together. If it involves visiting a local grocery store featuring food and other products from that cultural context, all the better. There is no quicker way to experience the reality of the world being at your doorstep than walking into a store and encountering different languages, sights, sounds, and smells. It may be enjoyable, it may be disorienting, but either way your family will certainly learn from the experience and strengthen their multiethnicity muscles.

As a side note, would doing so result in appropriating that

culture rather than appreciating it? What is the difference? What we described above is an example of appreciating a culture by getting to know it better and engaging in activities that will help deepen your understanding. There is never anything wrong with increasing your knowledge and that of your family. If, for example, you are ordering and enjoying Chinese food as a family, there is nothing inappropriate about trying to use chopsticks. But if your family has no direct connection to Chinese culture and your daughter wears a traditional Chinese dress as a Halloween costume, you will have crossed the line into appropriation: you are using elements of a different culture for your own—or, in this case, your daughter's— amusement and benefit. There are no hard-and-fast rules, but when in doubt, it's always better to err on the side of caution. While not every person of Chinese descent would be offended by the above scenario, some surely would be. And even if you have no intention of dishonoring another culture, part of growing in multiethnic awareness and understanding is recognizing that some people *will* feel dishonored by the inappropriate use of their cultural symbols. The loving thing to do is to put aside your own preferences and acknowledge that you might offend.

Convictions and Concerns

Have you heard the statement that the US is "a nation of immigrants"? This rings true for both of us: we are the daughters of immigrants. But to describe the US only in this way is to deny the true history of America as a land that was conquered, its host peoples largely eradicated and forcibly removed. This is just one example of the ways in which the narratives and mythologies that permeate our culture have been shaped by a dominant majority—one that preserves the idea of America as the land of equal opportunity and denies the reality that many ethnic groups have suffered oppression, discrimination, and enslavement at the hands of a white majority.

As you read the last paragraph, you might have found that you are in full agreement, or you might have found yourself cringing and resisting these statements. Part of increasing your multiethnic awareness is understanding why people of color and a growing number of white Americans believe our country is not a land of equal opportunity. If you neither fully understand nor agree with the earlier statements, please know that you are far from alone. Many American Christians struggle to think that the US is anything but a "Christian nation" and believe that God has truly blessed this country in ways he hasn't blessed others.

In fact, for both of us, it's this very mythology that led our parents to leave behind their respective countries of origin to seek out this "promised land." There is some truth to the idea that the US offered our parents opportunities that they couldn't have had otherwise.

But growing in multiethnic understanding means that you will begin to understand how the forces of injustice, discrimination, privilege, and wealth all had an impact on various ethnic groups here in the US in ways that continue to reverberate even today. It means that you will start to learn about American history from those whose stories haven't been readily available in our educational systems, a process requiring for many (the two of us included) a recalibration of our perspectives on our nation's heritage. And as we have mentioned often in this book, this type of growth and understanding comes with being intentional, willing to deconstruct your own assumptions and ideas, and open to learning from those on the margins who have a different story to tell those people who will take the time to listen. We hope you will be one of them.

From the numerous ways that Jesus changed the course of the historical narrative and upended people's understanding of power and justice, we can see that sometimes we need to be willing to throw out our previous ideas and embrace the mystery of God's kingdom, where the last will be first and the One who laid down his life for all is the Lord of all. What would the

US look like if more of our leaders, both inside and outside the church, embraced Jesus's example?

Practices for Assessing and Responding to Biases as a Race-Wise Family

Assessing your biases is more of a mental, soul-oriented exercise than some of our previous postures, and like many other processes that involve self-discovery and transformation, it will require dedicated time alone, with others, and with God. Here are practices that you can adopt as an individual or, where appropriate, with your family:

1. Take our Multiethnicity Quotient assessment (appendix 1) as a way to begin to understand your own areas of preference and bias. Encourage your spouse and high schoolers to take the assessment and discuss the results together. (You are free to make copies of the assessment and distribute them to your family members; you can also access an online version at wmbooks.com/racewiseextras.) Notice the areas where you and your family members scored low or high and what surprised or encouraged you.

2. As a family, pick one topic from the Multiethnicity Quotient a week to talk about over dinner. Ask the following questions:

   a. Did I observe bias today in myself or in others?
   b. What changes do I need to make to grow in my multiethnic awareness in this area?

3. Commit to retaking the assessment in six months to see where you have grown (or not) as individuals and as a family.

4. Google the brainteaser called "Here's a Riddle That Might Expose Your Blind Spot" with your elementary-aged and older children.[10] Although it is in reference to

gender bias, it helps illustrate the ways we can default to biases without even realizing it.

5. Watch instructive videos with your spouse, such as the implicit bias video series from UCLA[11] or Jennifer L. Eberhardt's TED Talk, "How Racial Bias Works—and How to Disrupt It,"[12] to better understand the sources of implicit and racial bias. Share with older children as appropriate so they can begin to learn the same concepts.

6. Ask people you know or encounter, especially people of color or people from other marginalized communities, to help you identify your biases. Give them permission to share with you any areas of bias they have noticed in you. Also, ask them whether they have had to battle particular stereotypes. For instance, I (Helen) feel as though I constantly have to contend with the stereotype that Asian women are docile, quiet, and meek. When I have a strong opinion about a particular topic, I am perceived to be much more assertive than I am really being. As you learn about potential areas of misunderstanding, your own propensity for bias will decrease.

7. Offer the following prayer either in your own devotional time or with your family:

God Who Sees,
We pray for clarity about the cultural and systemic influences
that shape our relationships, media choices, values, and habits.
We ask for greater awareness of our friend groups and
the ways we might be perpetuating systems and structures that
favor the dominant culture. Give us eyes to see our own limits
and shortcomings in order that we might become more open to
learning from others and shoring up our own areas of deficient
knowledge with the perspectives of those who can help us see you,
God, more fully and clearly.
Amen.

Journeying Toward Racial Healing

I (MICHELLE) WILL NEVER FORGET the first time I had to have "the talk" with my five-year-old son. He had overheard a conversation between my husband and me about Jacob Blake, a Black man who had been shot in Kenosha, Wisconsin. The police shot him seven times—in front of his children no less—leaving him paralyzed from the waist down. I hadn't realized my son was listening in as my husband and I grieved the incident. The look on my son's face immediately revealed that he understood the horrible weight of this tragedy.

It's hard to explain what it's like as a parent of color to witness your children being exposed to the horrors of racism in our country. We helplessly watch the heaviness of these situations sink slowly into their faces, their bodies, their emotions. It's not their shock you have to contend with but rather their fear and anger once they realize that people who look like them face this reality.

My son had a look of terror in his eyes. "Is that going to happen to my daddy?" he asked.

No matter how much you teach your kids about what to do and how to behave—how to not look "dangerous" and how to avoid looking suspicious in front of police—you can't shield them from racism in our country. They will both experience it firsthand and witness its impact on others. It often feels like no matter what we do, we will lose. If we stay silent, we get hurt. If we speak up, we get hurt. If we resist, we get hurt. If we don't resist, we get hurt. If we dress well, we get hurt. If we have a good job and are just trying to walk home after work, we get hurt. In an interview with ABC News, Blake said he resisted because he "didn't want to be the next George Floyd."[1]

Many of us have learned the hard truth that there is no magic formula that protects people of color in this country from becoming the victims of malicious, unjust attacks and other forms of racism. Unless something changes, our children will grow up watching the tragedy of Black and Brown bodies being shot in the streets and people from their communities being wrongly incarcerated, stereotyped, demonized, and more. As parents of color, many of us feel helpless at times because of what our children will encounter in the world.

To make matters even more complicated, the shooting of Jacob Blake happened as anti-Asian racism was escalating in our country, and I was navigating my own trauma and grief. I felt continually exhausted. There were days I didn't want to get out of bed or go to work or do anything for that matter. Asian Americans were reaching out from around the country for advice and someone to talk to, but I felt like I was barely able to care for myself, let alone others. Being a brown-skinned minority in this country means never fully being free of the pain of racism. I have a weight on my heart that never fully goes away, and with each new racial tragedy, that weight can sometimes feel debilitating. This was my current reality. This was my children's reality.

The day after the Blake shooting, I requested time off from work. It felt strange at first, asking for a day off due to racism, but my husband and friends encouraged me that taking time to care for my own mental and emotional health was important. I slept in, took a long shower, and then spent the day playing with my kids. We went for a walk and breathed in the fresh fall air. The sun was shining, and the warmth of the sun's rays felt healing. Rest and play were exactly what I needed on my journey of racial healing that day.

While this book as a whole is written for everyone, this chapter is written specifically for parents of color. As men and women of color, we carry our own pain from racism. We hold within us traumatic memories and experiences, not just of our own childhood but of our parents and our ancestors as well. When we add to this our country's larger racist past, our history and memory can feel like too great a weight to bear. Microaggressions, whether online or in person, can trigger us and unleash deep pain. Some of us are angry all the time, and others feel a continual melancholy in their souls. It's time we found healing not just for our sake but for the sake of our families and our children as well. Despite this current darkness, it is possible to experience the joy of the Lord (Nehemiah 8:10) and to pass on that joy to our children. If racial trauma can be passed from one generation to the next, joy can be passed down as well. In this chapter we will walk you and your family through biblical and practical steps to create safe spaces free of racism, so that together you may find healing and become resilient.

Defining Terms

Racial trauma or *race-based traumatic stress* "refers to the mental and emotional injury caused by encounters with racial bias and ethnic discrimination, racism, and hate crimes."[2] It is "the cumulative effects of racism on an individual's mental and physical health,"[3] which negatively impact one's overall well-being. A person of color suffering from racial trauma will have a hard time, emotionally and mentally, processing a racialized event. He or she may have nightmares about the event, greater anxiety, and increased sensitivity, fear, and/or lack of trust in people who look like the perpetrators involved in the racialized event.

Other effects include aggression, low self-image, shame, hyper-vigilance, pessimism, difficulty concentrating, substance abuse, flashbacks, and relational dysfunction. Racial trauma also contributes to heart disease, hyperactivity, and headaches.[4]

It's important to make space for big *T* and little *t* racial trauma. Most people of color experience both. It's not just a major national tragedy—like a shooting or a murder—that can be traumatic. Small, everyday microaggressions can build up and cause racial trauma. For example, continually being made fun of for speaking in Spanish, being the brunt of Asian or Native American jokes or receiving false compliments ("compli-insults") as an African American is like receiving a thousand paper cuts all over your body. These cuts hurt and are an attack against your dignity and personhood. But oftentimes when we show these cuts to others, they say, "Well, that's not so bad. It's not like you have a gaping hole or slash." In instances like this, we can lovingly respond (if we have the energy and capacity to) by simply saying, "No person of color should have to experience any form of racism, big or small. My pain and the trauma are real, and they shouldn't be discounted."

Racial healing is "[the ability] to heal from the wounds of the past [and] to build mutually respectful relationships across racial and ethnic lines that honor and value each person's humanity."[5] Racial healing doesn't mean we simply forget the pains of the past and move on. Rather, to pursue racial healing means to pursue wholeness. It's the ability to experience the love and peace of Jesus in the midst of a storm.

For people of color, racial healing is more of a journey than a destination because most of us will continue to experience the trauma, pain, and resilience cycle for the rest of our lives. To deal with our racial pain, we can cling to Jesus, go to therapy, take medication if we need it, and find practices and rhythms in life that bring stability to our emotional, mental, and physical health. That way, when the next microaggression or national tragedy occurs, we are better equipped to process and engage with it in a way that doesn't cause us to be as triggered as the last event.

Creating safe spaces is an important component in pursuing racial healing. A **safe space** is "a place or environment in which a person or category of people can feel confident that they will not be exposed to discrimination, criticism, harassment, or any other emotional or physical harm."[6] This could be your bedroom, your home in general, a garden, going camping out in nature, or spending time with a trusted friend. A safe space is a place of retreat. It's a place where we can dial down the noise of this world, hear our own thoughts and prayers, and practice soul care. It's also a place where we can ask for help.

A race-wise family must prioritize safe spaces so that both parents and children have regular opportunities to check in with one another. Perhaps this means creating a designated room in the house as the family's safe space. You might establish regular check-ins with each other, times when each family member can hear how the others are doing while being kind, considerate, and respectful of each other's pain and experiences. Healing is an intentional practice. If we desire racial healing for ourselves as well as for our children, we must be proactive about our family's overall health.

Creating Safe Spaces

It is paramount that we parents of color intentionally provide safe spaces where our families can openly acknowledge, process, and reflect on everything from racial tragedies to the racially motivated microaggressions we experience daily. Just as the COVID-19 pandemic was unfolding in spring 2020 and anti-Asian hatred was at its apex, I (Michelle) wrote an article for (in)courage. In it I noted the need for safe spaces:

> This is the model we see in Scripture. Time and again, men and women in both the Old and the New Testaments step away to find safety from the threats against their lives. Think of David and the many times he had to flee from King Saul. Notably, he found solace

in caves and remote spaces outside of the city. Think also of Elijah fleeing from Jezebel into the wilderness. He felt like he was completely alone, and the whole world was against him, but it was also in the wilderness where God meets him. Jesus, too, stepped away—not just to get away from the masses but to also flee verbal and physical threats. Think of His night in the Garden of Gethsemane. He pulled away to meet with God. He knew He was about to enter a fire storm, so He sought his Father's face for comfort.

There are many reasons why we need a physical space for retreat. We need them for our own physical, spiritual, and emotional safety.[7]

In fact, sometimes we need more than a temporary retreat. Sometimes we need to permanently remove our children from certain spaces for their own safety. My husband and I (Michelle) chose not to re-enroll our son in his preschool after he was the victim of racial bullying there. We must always consider the holistic safety of our children and whether their engagement in a certain space will be detrimental to their overall well-being. I said as much in my article:

> We need them [safe spaces] so we can seek out God. Whether that's our home, our bedroom, the park, or a nature trail, we need to know which spaces we can retreat to with the assurance of Matthew 1:23 that "God is with us" and that He will meet us in these places. . . . When we step away from the threats and pains of this world, we can pray that God will comfort our broken hearts and bind up our wounds (Psalm 147:3).[8]

Practically, the journey to racial healing means two things. First, we as parents need to have safe spaces, whether that's our homes or somewhere quiet outdoors, to practice soul care:

> These are spaces where we can find holistic rest—for us to close our eyes, go for a run, take care of our bodies, pull out a journal and reflect on our experiences, read our Bible and pray. It's

where we not only acknowledge the realities in our life but also lay them at Christ's feet and cast our cares upon Him.[9]

Feeling like you as a parent need to have your guard up all the time is exhausting. We need to cultivate space so that we can be honest with ourselves and give ourselves permission to express what we often hold in. Healing will come only when we choose to acknowledge, process, and reflect on the racialized pain we carry and then allow Christ to tenderly care for our hearts, bodies, and minds.

Second, we need to cultivate safe spaces with our children. What kinds of regular gatherings could we create that would give our families safe spaces to describe their experiences of and feelings about racism? When a racial tragedy grips our country, it's good to gather as a family and process together. These times should be a kind of listening session: you and your children can share your thoughts and emotions freely without having to explain or defend them. The goal is simply for everyone to have the opportunity to speak up, feel heard, and be validated. Here are some questions you can ask to open the conversation:

- How are you feeling about what happened?
- What have you seen and heard?
- How are your friends doing?
- What are you thinking about right now?

As you process the event together, remember that your healing and your children's healing are connected and related but not the same. Don't transfer your emotions to them. If your children are struggling to express their thoughts and feelings, read with them books on race and healing. Doing so helps them give language to their emotions, including sadness and rage. Moreover, let them know it's okay to express that sadness and anger. Also consider creating a welcoming environment by playing quiet, soothing music, providing soft blankets and pillows to

> **Healing will come only when we choose to acknowledge, process, and reflect on the racialized pain we carry and then allow Christ to tenderly care for our hearts, bodies, and minds.**

lounge on, and having some candles lit or a diffuser present. Special items and music help signal to your kids that this is a special place and time. It can also help them relax and feel more open to sharing what they're feeling. Finally, be aware that one safe space may not be enough for your children. They may need to open up to a therapist or counselor as well. Therapy is another safe and trusted environment where children can process what they're going through. Don't be afraid to explore this option with your kids.

It may be hard for you as a parent to feel comfortable sharing your emotions with either your spouse or your children. That's all right. These emotional muscles are strengthened with practice. "Write about it. Pray about it. It's okay to let the hurt in. We need to make space to verbally process the realities of racism and its impact on us."[10] When racial trauma happens in our country, it's wrong, and we need to have a place to verbally process these realities. We especially need to let our children feel seen and heard.

Talk. Journal. Pray together. Practice soul care as a family. Remember that "God sees you and He doesn't want you to carry the burden of racial oppression alone. Lay it at His feet, and believe that when you pray, 'Lord, heal me,' He will begin a process of healing within you."[11]

Foster Resilience

The goal of racial healing is resilience. As Sheila Wise Rowe wrote in her book *Healing Racial Trauma,*

> We need healing and new ways to navigate ongoing racism, systemic oppression, and racial trauma that impairs our ability to become more resilient. Resilience is the capacity to recover quickly from difficulties or to "work through them step by step, and bounce back stronger than you were before." In relation to racism, resilience refers to the ability "to persevere and maintain a positive sense of self when faced with omnipresent racial discrimination." Resilience is not an inherited trait; how we think, behave, and act can help us to grow in resilience.[12]

Rowe also argued that resilience means that we get well and we stay well.[13] This includes remembering what God has done and is doing in our lives, focusing on what we can change, and choosing to forgive. It also means staying strong in the face of racism, which will continue because of the sinfulness of our world. Our aim as race-wise families should be "to understand racial trauma, pursue healing, and build resilience to confront ongoing racism."[14]

Remember What God Has Done and Is Doing in Your Life

God cares about racism, and he is actively changing people's hearts and minds, my own included. Last year I (Michelle) wrote about this very topic in *Courageous Joy:* "I know myself. I'm quick to point out racism . . . I also need to make sure my radar is just as sensitive to the ways in which God sovereignly and graciously preserves the lives of people of color."[15]

It's always good for me to remember, "He has also raised up allies to expose and oppose systemic oppression against minorities."[16] Along with remembering and naming my allies, I need to "[spend] time in praise for the work God is doing in our churches and ministries, spaces that are no longer white-centered but Christ-centered, and that honor the lives and dignity of all peoples."[17]

Focus on What You Can Change

We need to be realistic. We won't be able to topple racist systems on our own. It's going to take a large number of people of all races telling their stories, sharing their lives, and challenging false narratives. But if we each choose to speak up and pursue love, peace, and justice in small and large ways, together we can begin to dismantle the systemic structures that promote racism. We each have a role to play, and we can commit to doing it to the best of our abilities.

Choose to Forgive

The more entrenched you become in the fight against racism, the more you open yourself up to becoming angry and bitter. But we have to choose forgiveness. According to Martin Luther King Jr., we have to fight for justice while loving the one doing the injustice,[18] and that's no easy task. First Peter 2:21–25 says that Jesus suffered on our behalf, leaving us an example: though he was reviled and slandered, he didn't slander in return. This fight against racism is hard, and the road is long. And we won't be able to survive, let alone thrive, if we don't continually ask God to protect our hearts and carry our burdens.

Practices to Journey Toward Racial Healing as a Race-Wise Family

As families of color navigating life in a world of racism, we have to continually ask ourselves, What feels heavy right now? What pain and trauma are we shouldering? What does healing look like? How can we grow in resilience? Here are some practical activities to do as you work through these questions. Take time this week to make a plan for soul care for both you and your children. You don't have to do everything on this list, but choose one or two activities that feel doable. Talk about them with your family and consider how you can begin implementing them today.

1. Make short-term and long-term plans for racial healing that are tailored to each of you as individuals based on your needs, resources, ability, and capacity. For example, a short-term plan could include encouraging your child to regularly journal about his feelings in order to both validate those feelings and reflect on his experiences. The short-term plan could also include "identifying things that make [her] feel calm, like specific music, food, spaces, or visuals and talk[ing] about how to access those things during a moment of need."[19] A long-term plan could involve helping your child learn how to calmly talk about racial incidents and experiences through the use of certain phrasing (e.g., "I am angry because . . .") as well as how to use breathing techniques and prayer. We each have different experiences and needs. The best thing we can do for ourselves and for our children is to honor one another's experiences.

2. Take care of your body and your children's bodies. We know that racial trauma affects our health, causing migraines, back pain, ulcers, and more. An important first step to holistic care is doing your best to make sure your whole family is eating healthy food, getting good sleep,

and keeping physically active. Spend time this week looking over your grocery list and meal plans. Schedule time to go for a run, a walk, or even a swim or bike ride as a family too.

3. Identify people you can trust. Seek support and help from family members and friends. Talk with your children about who those people are. Provide their contact information for your children if they are older and can use a phone. Consider going to a counselor as well. Each of you needs space to share what you are experiencing, to process emotions, and to rebuild feelings of worthiness and belonging.

4. Create healthy boundaries. Identify specific people or places that continue to trigger racial pain for your family. Then determine what is necessary to maintain a healthy distance from them.

5. Make space for humor and laughter. Watch a funny movie together. Look up silly jokes or do Mad Libs. Being playful despite racial pain can be a powerful way to strengthen your family bonds and relieve the stress of the moment.

6. Develop relaxation exercises. Whether it's praying, listening to a calming audiobook, doing stretches, or pausing for a moment to take deep breaths, we need to find slow, gentle activities to help relieve the racially induced stress we experience.

7. If you are a white parent and/or the parent of white children, you can encourage your family to be allies to families of color by texting or calling to check in and let them know you're thinking of them especially in the aftermath of a racial tragedy. You can also offer help in a time of crisis—and respect if their answer is no. Also, you can talk to your own children about racial pain and trauma and encourage them to educate their white peers about racism and allyship as well. Finally, you can ask

questions out of curiosity (as opposed to making accusations) and practice empathy without overidentifying or centering yourself in the situation.

8. Offer the following prayer either in your own devotional time or with your family:

God Who Blesses the Poor in Spirit,
You know, dear Lord, how much pain there is in the world today,
how the evil of racism and bigotry in all its forms has left wounds
in the hearts, minds, and souls of so many people of color.
Please send your Spirit to heal all those who suffer, to be
the Great Physician for those who are despairing and hurting
today. Help the body of Christ to be sensitive to the pain of those
who are marginalized and suffering and to respond with kindness,
grace, and mercy. As all creation groans for complete restoration,
give your people the patience to persevere through hardships.
May we know your love and goodness even in our heartache.
May we choose to praise you and your mighty deeds with faith
and hope, trusting that you will bring your good work to
completion in the last days. May your name be lifted up
and may your justice roll down, bringing relief and
redemption to our broken and divided world.
Amen.

Raising Kingdom-Minded Children

IN THE SUMMER OF 2020, the nation was aflame with protests in the wake of the murders of George Floyd, Ahmaud Arbery, and Breonna Taylor, and social media platforms were full of posts heralding that Black lives matter and expressing outrage about the current state of racial injustice. I (Helen) noticed that all three of my boys had used their Instagram accounts to join in the chorus. I asked my twelve-year-old (youngest) son about his decision to do so. "Well, everyone else was doing it, so I thought I should too," he responded. Although I was glad that he and his brothers had their eyes open to what was happening around them, I was concerned that my son's reasons for posting on Instagram weren't ideal.

Standing against racial injustice is part of our Christian witness, but if our children are driven more by a desire to conform to the cultural moment than by kingdom-minded values, they won't have the wisdom to do what is right even when it is unpopular to do so.

As Christians, we regularly pray as Jesus taught us, "Thy kingdom come, thy will be done in earth, as it is in heaven" (Matthew 6:10, KJV). In other words, not only are we praying in

> **Standing against racial injustice is part of our Christian witness, but if our children are driven more by a desire to conform to the cultural moment than by kingdom-minded values, they won't have the wisdom to do what is right even when it is unpopular to do so.**

expectation of a future reality once Jesus has returned, but we're also praying boldly for a present reality that bears witness to this hope. And we're expressing our willingness to be part of bringing that reality into the present—we're not just asking God to make things right in our nation and world while we sit idly by and watch him work. When it comes to issues of race, we're acknowledging that there is work to be done here on earth and that we're submitting to God's leadership in establishing his rule in the present day. But there are important principles to keep in mind as we strive to build race-wise families in a kingdom-minded manner. Especially in this day and age when many more people are engaging in discussions about race, it is easy to lose sight of what it means to pursue racial awareness and justice in a God-honoring way. There is a difference between being race-aware and race-wise, and the posture of kingdom-mindedness makes the difference.

Defining Terms

To understand what it means to be kingdom-minded, it helps to first understand what it means to be **culture-conforming**. Often without even realizing it, we're being shaped by invisible cultural forces all around us. If either of us had grown up in India or South Korea instead of the United States, even though our genetic makeup would have been exactly the same, we would have grown up to be completely different people. Such is the shaping power of culture.

The challenge for us Christians is to recognize when we're conforming to the culture around us in ways that don't honor God. If we're a member of any dominant cultural group, we're more susceptible to having our thinking and beliefs shaped by that group. Although demographics are shifting in the US, the movers and shakers of our country are still predominantly white in every major culture-shaping context (e.g., politics, the media, arts and entertainment, educational institutions, the church).[1] This reality affects the air that we all breathe; it creates the unwritten rules that govern our cultural norms, ideals, and expectations. Whatever the cultural norms are, we are expected to conform, and the invisible pressures to do so are inexorably strong.

This is true especially in the area of race. David Swanson, author of *Rediscipling the White Church*, noted that for white Christians in particular, white culture has shaped parents and children without their even realizing it. I (Helen) was discussing this very topic with David recently when he said,

> Our churches do not disciple white Christians away from racial segregation and injustice. Our children are constantly observing and interpreting our racialized culture. White Christianity's silence about issues like privilege, racism, and segregation amounts to abandoning them to the deforming discipleship of our racially unjust society.[2]

As Christians, we need to be mindful of these invisible forces that have shaped and continue to shape the way we think and live. There is a reason that Paul admonished us in Romans 12:2 to "not conform to the pattern of this world, but be transformed by the renewing of your mind. Then you will be able to test and approve what God's will is—his good, pleasing and perfect will." The antidote, then, to conforming to culture

> **Being kingdom-
> minded means that
> we acknowledge the
> spiritual war happening
> within and around us, and
> we realize that if we aren't
> alert, we will actually be
> serving the Enemy rather
> than the King.**

is "the renewing of your mind"—or, as we're calling it, kingdom-mindedness.

What does it mean to be kingdom-minded? We define **kingdom-mindedness** as recognizing the rule of God Almighty over all and choosing to humbly submit ourselves as followers of Jesus. In contrast to being culture-conforming, being kingdom-minded means that we understand that sin always leads us away from the kingdom and toward the patterns of the culture that surrounds us. Being kingdom-minded also means that we acknowledge the spiritual war happening within and around us, and we realize that if we aren't alert, we will actually be serving the Enemy rather than the King.

Kingdom-mindedness doesn't happen automatically by virtue of being a Christian. It requires a daily submission to Jesus, it is a minute-by-minute journey, and—truth be told—we often fail especially in the area of being race-wise when so many voices are swirling around us, telling us what we should think and how we should act. But if we are kingdom-minded, then serving the King of kings is our highest aspiration, and we desire to be transformed more and more into his likeness, made more and more worthy of being citizens of heaven.

Biblical Principles of Kingdom-Mindedness

Where do we begin our journey to becoming kingdom-minded? We should first help our children understand what it means to approach our heavenly King with a posture of fear and trembling because of all that he has done and all that he will do in his good and perfect time. This fear and trembling isn't the same as being scared of God. C. S. Lewis wonderfully depicted the difference in his classic book *The Lion, the Witch and the Wardrobe* with this description of Aslan, the great Lion:

> "Ooh!" said Susan, "I'd thought he was a man. Is he—quite safe? I shall feel rather nervous about meeting a lion."
>
> "That you will, dearie, and no mistake," said Mrs. Beaver; "if there's anyone who can appear before Aslan without their knees knocking, they're either braver than most or else just silly."
>
> "Then he isn't safe?" said Lucy.
>
> "Safe?" said Mr. Beaver; "don't you hear what Mrs. Beaver tells you? Who said anything about safe? 'Course he isn't safe. But he's good. He's the King, I tell you."[3]

This is a difficult concept for us—parents and children alike—to understand because there is no real human equivalent. Even if we were to stand before the president of the United States, for example, we might experience nerves but not the kind of knee-knocking fear that Lewis described. Yet the Bible tells us that "the fear of the LORD is the beginning of wisdom, and knowledge of the Holy One is understanding" (Proverbs 9:10). So to gain a fuller knowledge of what it means to refuse to conform to culture, we must begin on our knees, asking for wisdom in holy fear and reverence. Our kids need to see us doing this, both literally and figuratively. We can't trust in our own limited understanding alone. Instead, we need to humbly and fully rely on God's infinite grace, mercy, and love.

At my (Helen's) house, Romans 12:2 is displayed on

> **If we are kingdom-minded, serving the King of kings is our highest aspiration, and we desire to be transformed more and more into his likeness, made more and more worthy of being citizens of heaven.**

> **We can't trust in our own limited understanding alone. Instead, we need to humbly and fully rely on God's infinite grace, mercy, and love.**

a printed card on the refrigerator door. Multiple times a day the whole family can see its reminder to stand against cultural conformity. Deuteronomy 6 instructs parents to talk about God's commandments "when you sit at home and when you walk along the road, when you lie down and when you get up" (verse 7), which essentially means all the time. In other words, the best way to stand firm in the Lord and embrace kingdom-minded living is to keep God at the center of what you do and say as much as is humanly possible. There is no way you can talk about God too much, even if your kids might tell you that you do!

We can also learn key principles from Jesus and his disciples, who modeled what it means to evangelize about the kingdom of God by focusing on the message of repentance and providing physical and spiritual healing (Matthew 10:1–42; Mark 6:6–13). We, too, must begin with repentance: it is a key part of our witness as race-wise families. We parents have to own our personal mistakes in the area of race and admit them to our children so they, too, can learn from those mistakes. Perhaps we spoke hurtful words or affirmed racist ideas. Maybe we had the chance to speak up when someone was being victimized by racial taunts, and we did nothing. Perhaps the Lord has been impressing on us the ways we haven't fully embraced the *imago Dei* in those who are ethnically and racially different from us. Or maybe we are learning about our own complicity—through action or inaction—in keeping whiteness embedded in our schools, workplaces, churches, and communities, and we have reacted defensively when a Christian of color has tried to point out our errors. We have to be honest with our kids about the ways we have fallen short of God's ideals and then help them see that we are repenting and seeking to be healed of our own areas of race-related brokenness.

Next, we have to recognize that the racist systems and structures around us are a result of the brokenness of this world and of the sin that exists in every human heart. So we are talking about a problem that is spiritual at the core, one that requires spiritual healing and transformation. This is why the body of Christ is the only entity that has a hope of truly addressing and dismantling racial injustice and racism in all its forms. And being kingdom-minded about the way we approach issues of race means that we acknowledge the spiritual nature of these issues and continually pray for healing in ourselves, in our families and communities, and in our nation and world.

As we pray with our kids about race-related issues, we can explain to them how necessary our prayers are as we battle "the powers of this dark world and . . . the spiritual forces of evil in the heavenly realms" (Ephesians 6:12). I (Helen) might have doubted the purity of my youngest son's motivation when he followed the crowd in posting on social media, but I had no doubts about his sincerity when he asked God to stop the killings of Black people in America during a time of family devotions. "That is a big way you can help battle racism," I told him. "Your prayers matter."

Last, in a simple directive, the Bible clearly lays out our calling as Christ followers: "Seek first [God's] kingdom and his righteousness" (Matthew 6:33). In other words, we are citizens of heaven before we are citizens of any nation. Our identity as citizens of God's kingdom must take priority over any other allegiances or convictions, even our ethnicity and race. But being citizens of heaven doesn't mean that we automatically

> **Our identity as citizens of God's kingdom must take priority over any other allegiances or convictions, even our ethnicity and race.**

understand what God's kingdom is about. There is a reason why Jesus spoke in parables: these stories about God's kingdom demonstrated that work was required on the part of the listener to decipher what Jesus was saying (Matthew 13:10–12). Jesus wasn't just spoon-feeding people information about the kingdom; he was testing to see who truly wanted to make the effort of seeking a fuller understanding of this kingdom. So it is with us today. If you want to be kingdom-minded—and if you want to truly understand issues of race and how they manifest today—you have to be willing to pursue that understanding, wrestle with these issues, and come to your own conclusions. And as you let your kids see that you are wrestling, that you don't have all the answers, that you are seeking the Lord's wisdom and direction as to how to approach issues of race, they will learn the importance of engaging in this process.

Barriers to Kingdom-Mindedness

When you humbly submit yourself to God and to a pursuit of his kingdom, you will soon discover that the process won't be smooth. You will face opposition, criticism, and backlash, and sometimes the strongest critics will be fellow believers. Division is one of the ways Satan seeks to confuse and destroy the church of Jesus Christ. But criticism isn't evidence that you are straying from God's intended path. In fact, we would say the opposite: seeking after the kingdom means that you absolutely will become a target of other Christians who don't fully understand, whose eyes are still blind to the spiritual sickness in themselves and in our nation.

You may also hear that journeying into a deeper understanding of racial sin in the nation, the church, or our own families will just lead to division. This may well be true. But when Jesus prayed that we would be one (John 17:20–23), he wasn't asking that we would be of the same mind on all issues. Earlier he said that the world would know we are Christians by our love

> Fear not if you experience opposition as you grow in your understanding of issues of race. Think of those moments as opportunities to demonstrate the love of Christ, which is the best witness we can have in a world that is fractured and polarized.

for one another (John 13:35) *even if we don't agree on everything*, which we surely won't. What marks us as Christians isn't that we have complete unity of thought on every issue; it is that we seek to love one another despite our differences. *That* is what will show the rest of the world that we are truly followers of Jesus. So, fear not if you experience opposition as you grow in your understanding of issues of race. Think of those moments as opportunities to demonstrate the love of Christ, which is the best witness we can have in a world that is fractured and polarized.

Practices to Cultivate Kingdom-Minded Living as a Race-Wise Family

What practices can you incorporate into your family rhythms that will lead you toward kingdom-minded living? And how will these practices help you become more race-wise parents and kids?

1. Stop. Then pray. In this day and age, when it seems as though everybody is expressing outrage over incidents of racism, it can be easy to feel as though the right thing to do is to add your voice to the mix. But the kingdom-minded approach is not just to follow the masses, to conform to the culture. Instead, it is to take the time to stop and reflect on those impulses, bring them before the Lord, and acknowledge your own propensity to err in this area. With a posture of humility and repentance, ask the

Lord to show you your blind spots. Then ask him, *What would you have me/us say or do in response to this injustice and evil?*

2. Organize times of "praying in one voice" with other Christians. In Korean culture, Christians often gather to pray out loud at the same time. It's a powerful way to experience solidarity as we collectively cry out to God. Either you can do something similar in your own family or church context, or you can invite friends, other families, or church members to commit to praying about race-related issues in their own way at an appointed time.

3. Commit to regularly attend a lecture or other event featuring a person of color. It could be every month, every quarter, or whatever you can manage in your schedule. But make this a consistent practice and invite your family members to go along to age-appropriate events. Libraries and bookstores feature authors on a regular basis, and with webinars and online conferences, there is no end to the number of ways available to learn from people of color. Being kingdom-minded means that you will continue to sit at the feet of Jesus and learn from those he brings into your life.

I (Helen) remember the day when I saw that the Newbery Medal–winning poet and novelist Kwame Alexander—whose content my junior higher Sean had just started reading—was coming to a bookstore in a neighboring town. Taking Sean to hear Alexander and delighting together in his skills, creative genius, and larger-than-life personality probably did more to form Sean's understanding of Black men than anything I could have told him. Also, it was important for Sean to see how much I enjoyed sitting and learning at the feet of a Black man. We all need to keep pursuing the healthy race-wise posture of letting people of color be our teachers.

4. As a family, use arts and crafts to create tangible expressions of what you are learning. For example, you can make a collage celebrating your growth as a race-wise family. Collaging is a form of artistic expression that anyone of any age can participate in.

   Spend a Sabbath afternoon together making a list of the key people and historical and current events you have learned about on your journey of racial understanding, and print out pictures, news articles, or web pages to cut out and use in the collage. On a piece of poster board or two, affix all the images and clippings you have gathered. (If your family wants to make a more permanent collage, you can get materials at your local craft store such as water-based sealer and stiffer poster board.)

   You can also gather inspiring quotes by people of color and turn those quotes into posters that you can print in your own home and frame. Online design programs like Canva make it easy to create posters that look professionally designed even if you have no design experience. (My husband and I find that our kids are usually quite good with these online programs given that they are digital natives!)

   Displaying these kinds of crafts in your house turns them into conversation starters when friends and family visit and gives you a way to share about your family's growth in understanding issues of race.

5. Give testimonies of what you are learning about race-wise living at your church or with family and friends. In fact, the most powerful testimonies can come from our kids. Jesus made it clear that we become kingdom-minded when we are willing to become like children (Matthew 18:3). What does this mean? From our experience, we find that children are open to truths about God and willing to engage in conversations about tough topics in ways that many adults aren't. Culture has had less

time to pressure our kids to conform, so they can often adopt kingdom-minded postures more easily than adults can.

I (Helen) remember when my eldest, who was thirteen years old at the time, was preparing his testimony for his confirmation service. To set up the story of God's work in his life, our son wanted to share about times when he had experienced racial bullying. To be quite frank, my first response was anxiety as I thought about our predominantly white church congregation with its range of attitudes and opinions on the topic of race. But he had no doubts about doing so, and I trusted his instincts and the leading of God's Spirit as he crafted and shared his story. In the end, his testimony helped open the eyes of those in the church who seemed to believe that race was no longer an issue, and because it was a young person speaking, the adults who otherwise might have been closed to the topic demonstrated a willingness to hear and understand. Such is the powerful way in which God can use our children as they embrace a kingdom-minded posture regarding race.

6. Invite others to join your journey. Community is key to being able to stay on this path for the long haul. Anything you strive to do that pushes against cultural tides—and kingdom-minded living absolutely falls into this category—will require superhuman strength to maintain over time. It's possible that an individual Christian could manage it, but this isn't the way God intends his people to make their way through life. We know it can be so, so hard to be in any way involved in this kind of work. But we also know that we aren't alone, though we have both experienced the isolating nature of kingdom-minded antiracism endeavors.

If you are on this journey alone, either as an individual or as a married couple, pray for others with whom you can walk this course. You don't need a huge group of like-minded people; it's enough to have even one friend who shares your conviction that kingdom-mindedness is the proper posture from which to address racial issues and attack racial injustices. If you can't find people in proximity to you who can be a support network, you can surely find them online, thanks to social media. It's not the same as experiencing embodied relationships, of course, but at the very least, as you find people online to follow, learn from, and be inspired by, you will discover that you are far from alone.

7. Offer this prayer either in your own devotional time or with your family:

> *God of the New Heaven and New Earth,*
> *Help us not to conform to the culture around us but to be*
> *kingdom-minded in all we do as individuals and as parents.*
> *Give us the wisdom to lead our families in a manner that reflects*
> *your values and your mission. Protect us from the Evil One, who*
> *would endeavor to confuse our minds and lead us astray. May our*
> *lives reflect the saving work of Jesus so that others will be drawn*
> *to you, especially because of how we handle issues related to race.*
> *Thank you for creating a way for all the nations to be adopted*
> *into your family and thank you that we have access to your*
> *kingdom through the shed blood of the King of kings, Jesus Christ.*
> *May we be single-minded in our devotion to our Savior*
> *until he comes again to reign forevermore.*
> *Amen.*

Epilogue

Our Prayer Until Jesus Comes

WE HAVE COME to the close of our ten postures of a race-wise family, and in some ways we are ending at the beginning. Everything we do in this area as individuals and as parents flows from the posture of seeking after the kingdom of God and the kingdom principles that shape our priorities, commitments, convictions, and perspectives. We are in a lifelong struggle against the power of evil, but we can rest in the assurance that all evil—including racism in all its overt and covert forms—will be destroyed no matter how hard the journey may be to get there. As stated throughout the book, we are headed toward a multiethnic, multilingual community that displays the incredible diversity of God's human creation yet is unified in devotion to our heavenly King (Revelation 7:9–10).

As the Holy Spirit shapes our minds and hearts and as we take Jesus's message of repentance, healing, hope, and restoration to every tongue, tribe, and nation, our witness will help further the kingdom of God. May we and our children and our children's children pursue this kingdom in a manner that allows us to stand before God at the end of our lives knowing that we were obedient to his call and that our lives helped draw more people to his kingdom. This is our prayer for you—and it is our prayer for ourselves and our families—until Jesus comes to restore our broken world and make it into a new creation where there is no more crying, dying, or hurting.

Let it be so, Lord.

Acknowledgments

THE WORDS ON THESE PAGES were written during a global pandemic, during the aftermath of the March 16 Atlanta massacre in which six Asian women were killed. Numerous other national and local crises—including a winter storm that shut down my East Austin community for several weeks—were also unfolding. I am grateful, first and foremost, for God's hand of grace and strength over both Helen and me and for the ways he equipped us to persevere during such a difficult year.

There are many people I want to thank for their emotional and intellectual support throughout this journey. First, Aaron, my husband. Thank you, love, for your unshakable support and for numerous evenings spent on our living room couch talking about what it means to be a race-wise family. I hope every married author is blessed to have a spouse who encourages, supports, and dialogues about their projects the way Aaron does with me.

I am grateful for the ever-continuing encouragement from my Asian American sisters Dorina Gilmore-Young, Tasha Jun Burgoyne, and Grace Cho who spent countless hours over Voxer and text offering valuable insights and feedback. I'm thankful for Dorena Williamson, who shares a heart for pursuing diversity and healing within the body of God. Her support over this past year has been a balm. Thank you, Cristal Porter and Jessica Darnell, for your friendship and support here in Austin. Thank you for inviting me to open up about the ideas in this book and to hear stories from your own families of what it means to be race-wise. Thank you for also watching my children at times so I could just hunker down and write.

I am also indebted to the support of my church, Hope Community Church. As scholar in residence, I have had the opportunity to work out my ideas at church through personal conversations, teaching, writing, and town halls. The men and women at Hope, including the staff and elders, have asked useful questions and helped me flesh out some of my ideas. There is no question that my church believes in me, in my giftings and passions, and I feel keenly their support of my writing journey.

Thank you to Don Gates, my agent, and to Chris Park, Helen's agent, for your support. Don and Chris have been an amazing agent duo, and it has been a joy to collaborate as a foursome—Don, Chris, Helen, and me—for this project.

Last but not least, I want to thank WaterBrook for publishing this book. You saw the importance and timeliness of a book on being a race-wise family and have been nothing but supportive on this journey. Thank you for moving the needle forward in publishing women of color and especially in supporting the voices of Asian American women in conversations on race.

—Michelle Ami Reyes

This has been a project a long time in coming. I've been thinking about it in one way or another for nearly a decade, but it wasn't until I connected with Michelle Reyes in person at the Someday Is Here conference in 2019—right before the world shut down—that the path to writing this book became clear.

Thank you, Michelle, for saying yes to this project and taking the leap of faith to partner together. You have been a delight to work with in bringing this book to life! The project has been a lifeline amid the dark days of the pandemic and the even darker days of racial unrest and tension, all the anti-Asian hatred we had to witness and experience, and continuing race-related struggles in the church.

Speaking of Someday Is Here, I owe a debt to my longtime friend Vivian Mabuni for bringing Michelle and me together. Thank you for your committed heart and your faithfulness to the mission God has given you to help raise the next generation of Asian American women. I couldn't have written this book without the Korean sisterhood that has provided me with solidarity and support for so many years: Angie, Irene, and Kathy, I appreciate your friendship more than you know!

I have learned much from so many fellow authors, writers, colleagues, and friends, especially through my work at both InterVarsity Press and previously at Missio Alliance. Terumi Echols, Jeff Crosby, and Lisa Rodriguez-Watson merit particular recognition for their support for my perspectives and convictions as a woman of color. There are too many other people to mention by name here, but for all of you who have graciously and prophetically tackled the topics of race, ethnicity, and identity, following God's call to preach a holistic gospel that furthers God's reconciling message of hope and healing: thank you. This work is not easy, it makes you vulnerable to critique and condemnation especially from others within the church, and it can be exhausting. But God sees your efforts and the risks you take for the furthering of his kingdom, and I am grateful for your work.

I've been blessed to produce *The Every Voice Now Podcast* and *The Disrupters* podcast over this past year, and it has been a deep source of joy to hear the stories from so many authors of color and how they persevered in their publishing journeys. Sometimes when I was struggling with what to say or do with this project, I would hear just the right nugget I needed from the guest of the week. Thank you to all these authors of color for your faithfulness and for sharing your stories!

I, too, want to offer thanks to Don Gates for the positive energy he has brought to this project and to my longtime agent, Chris Park, who still stands by me and offers invaluable support and advice whenever I need it. You're the best, Chris!

Becky Nesbitt, you have been a fabulous editor to work with; your kindness and conscientiousness have made you a model of editorial excellence. As a former book marketer myself, I appreciate all the efforts from the WaterBrook marketing team, including but not limited to Johanna Inwood and Brett Benson. Thank you for your hard work that often goes unseen and underrecognized! Laura Barker, your commitment to this project from the start has been such an encouragement. And to the countless people at WaterBrook who have touched this project and whose work has contributed to it, even though their names are not listed here, I am grateful for your excellent work!

I've appreciated the ways my church, Naperville Covenant Church, has been willing to tackle the difficult topic of race and to give me the chance to work through a number of the issues we have written about here. Thanks to Scot and Meagan Gillan, Kelly Johnston, and Leslie X. Sanders for being such helpful conversation and ministry partners over the years.

I couldn't write a book on the race-wise family without mentioning my own: my three sons—Jason, Sean, and Aidan—have borne the brunt of my ignorance and missteps in this area, and they have also been gracious and open to our many conversations about these challenging topics. I will continue to pray that God uses your lives to bring his reconciling hope and healing to those around you! My husband, Brian, helps me see all the different angles of these complicated questions, and I appreciate his steadfast heart and his commitment to honor and pursue God and his kingdom in all he does, which inspires me to do the same. Much love to my FamiLee!

—Helen Lee

The Multiethnicity Quotient Assessment

We want to provide you with a tool to easily assess the multiethnicity quotient of your own life. You are welcome to make copies and share them with others. We highly recommend that both you and your spouse or other significant family caregiver(s) take this assessment. (You can also go to wmbooks.com/race wiseextras to score this assessment online and receive tailored recommendations and resources.)

Read through the following statements. If you agree with the statement, give yourself two points. If the statement applies to you only sometimes, give yourself one point. Tally each section separately, and then total all five sections for your final score. These questions are geared toward families and assume that at least one parent and one child are in the household.

Community

1. In my nuclear and/or immediate extended family, different ethnicities are represented.

2. When I think of my six closest friends, at least half of them are from a different ethnic group than mine.
3. My neighborhood is at least 20 percent non-white.
4. My child/children have at least one person of a different ethnicity in their group of closest friends.
5. When I look at my five closest neighbors, at least two of them are from a different ethnic group than mine.
6. The organization where I work or where my spouse works is at least 20 percent non-white.
7. I have had training in cross-cultural communication.
8. I have had to code-switch in order to communicate effectively in different contexts.
9. I appreciate relational styles that are different from my own.
10. I have experienced conflict resolution with someone from a different ethnic background.

Community Total Score: _____

Consumerism

1. Of the last five books I've read, at least two were by authors of color.
2. When I think about my five favorite books, at least two are by authors of color.
3. When I think about my child/children's five favorite books, at least two feature lead characters of color.
4. When I think about my five favorite television shows from this past year, at least one features a diverse cast.
5. I have watched a foreign-language film in the past year.
6. When I think about my ten favorite musicians, at least three are artists of color.
7. I intentionally watch television shows or movies featuring people who are different from me and contexts that are unfamiliar to me.

8. I notice when people of color are missing from popular culture that I consume.
9. I can name ten actors of color, five who are African American and five who are from other ethnic backgrounds.
10. I have watched at least two films featuring a non-white cast in the past two years.

Consumerism Total Score: _____

Christian Living

1. The church I attend is at least 30 percent non-white.
2. My family chose our church because of its ethnic composition.
3. Our church displays a range of worship styles from a variety of cultures.
4. People of color are onstage or in the pulpit every Sunday at our church.
5. My child/children regularly learn from people of color in Sunday school.
6. Our church takes time to lament racial injustice.
7. I have attended at least two Christian conferences in person or online with a majority non-white speaker list.
8. I have attended at least two Christian conferences in person or online with a group of majority non-white attendees.
9. When I think of the five most influential Christians I follow, read, or listen to, at least two are people of color.
10. I regularly tune in to sermons from pastors or other leaders who are non-white.

Christian Living Total Score: _____

Cross-Cultural Competency

1. I regularly eat food from ethnic backgrounds that are not my own.
2. When I think about my five favorite restaurants, at least two are from a culture that is not my own.
3. I have given my child/children regular exposure to foods from different cultures.
4. I intentionally do not call food from other cultures "ethnic foods."
5. I am familiar with at least two languages that are not my native tongue.
6. In the past year, I have eaten food that was unfamiliar to me and that I was uncomfortable with.
7. I have traveled to at least two countries outside the US, not including Canada and Mexico.
8. I enjoy getting to know cultural contexts that I am not familiar with.
9. In the past month, I have been to a grocery store featuring a non-white cultural context.
10. I regularly watch travel shows featuring different cultural contexts.

Cross-Cultural Competency Total Score: _____

Convictions and Concerns

1. I understand why more and more states are denouncing Columbus Day as an official holiday.
2. I grieve over our nation's history of mistreating people of color, especially indigenous people groups and African Americans.
3. I am aware that, until 1965, laws restricting immigration from Asian nations were in effect.

4. I recognize that calling the US "a nation of immigrants" does not accurately reflect that there are people groups who are indigenous to our country.
5. I understand the terms *Jim Crow* and *the new Jim Crow*.
6. Regardless of my political leanings, I can celebrate when glass ceilings are broken in politics.
7. When I see examples of police brutality toward African Americans, I grieve over those instances of injustice.
8. I talk with my child/children about current events that have a racial dimension.
9. I understand the impact that NAFTA had on the economic situation in Mexico and the ramifications for immigration from that country.
10. I am aware that US restrictions on refugees have become increasingly and overly stringent over the years.

Convictions and Concerns Total Score: _____

Total Multiethnicity Quotient: _____

Scoring (out of 100)

90-100: Strong

If you scored 90 points or above, it is clear that you value multiethnicity and that it is woven into your life. The next step for you would be to ask yourself whether your family as a whole would rate as highly as you have. If not, what areas are weaker than others, and what can you do to strengthen those areas? Also, consider your extended family members and friends. How can you be an influence in their lives so that they will see that you value multiethnicity and will be inspired or challenged to do the same?

75-89: Encouraging

If you scored in this range, you are on the right path to creating and sustaining a multiethnic life, but you have room for improvement. Reaching the next level will require intentionality and effort; otherwise you could stay at this level for the foreseeable future. But if you lean in and choose to deepen your commitment to multiethnicity, you will see dividends not only in your own life but also in your children's lives over time.

60–74: On Your Way

You value multiethnicity on some level, but there are many areas in your life where you could increase your understanding of and commitment to multiethnic issues. While you could stay at this level without any extreme ramifications to yourself or your family, you will be missing out on more fully relating to people who are different from you, both in the body of Christ and beyond.

Below 60: Room for Improvement

Multiethnicity may still be a fairly foreign or distant concept for you. The good news is, by reading this book and beginning to deepen your understanding of race, you are already on the path to greater knowledge about multiethnicity and the value of living a multiethnic life. Ask the Lord to show you which area you can start making changes to, consider the suggestions in appendixes 3 and 5, and periodically reassess yourself to see how you are increasing your Multiethnicity Quotient.

Kid-Friendly Definitions

Ally: An ally is someone who isn't directly impacted by an issue but is willing to show up in solidarity for that issue.

Code-switching: People code-switch when they change how they talk and act based on whom they are with. For example, a person's words to a teacher might be different from her words to her best friend; similarly, her words to someone from her culture might be different from her words to someone from a different culture.

Compassion: Compassion is feeling someone else's pain and then doing your best to relieve that person's suffering.

Critical race theory: A movement stemming from legal studies, critical race theory argues that many of the laws and systems in the United States are racist and therefore disadvantage non-white people, both historically and in the present.

Culture: Culture is a person's way of life, including his or her stories, values, and activities.

Cultural competence: Cultural competence is the ability to connect with people of different cultures. It requires both knowing and appreciating the unique aspects of a person's culture.

Cultural identity: Cultural identity refers to the stories we inherit and create about ourselves based on our ethnic roots.

Cultural representation: Cultural representation is the idea that the multiethnic range of people should be reflected throughout relevant social systems and structures.

Discrimination: Discrimination is the act of seeing or treating someone negatively based on some aspect of his or her identity (skin color, weight, physical features, etc.).

Disprivilege: Disprivilege is when someone has been deprived of a privilege.

Diversity: Diversity is the result of intentionally including people from a range of racial, cultural, and ethnic backgrounds.

Empathy: Empathy is the ability to feel or experience what someone else is going through.

Equality: Equality means that every person is treated with the same dignity and worth.

Equity: Equity is creating systems and processes that ensure everyone has equal opportunity to succeed.

Ethnicity: Ethnicity refers to our roots, and it encompasses our racial, national, tribal, religious, linguistic, and cultural origins.

Gospel-rooted news literacy: Having gospel-rooted news literacy means that after we watch the news, we ask ourselves, *How* *would God want me to respond to this situation?* We find the answer to this question through praying and reading God's Word.

Intersectionality: The idea behind intersectionality is that people are complex human beings. Our gender, race, class, sex, ability, religion, etc. are all part of who we are. Each of us lives at the intersection of these different identities.

Lament: Lament is when we grieve over a painful experience while also believing that God will take care of us.

Microaggression: A microaggression is any subtle expression—including words, facial expressions, and behaviors—that conveys hurtful ideas about race toward a racial minority.

Multicultural: Multicultural means the equal presence of and value for more than one distinct cultural group and their different worldviews, behaviors, values, and traditions.

Multiethnicity: Multiethnicity means a collection of more than one ethnic group in any given space.

Narrative justice: Narrative justice means finding ways to elevate the stories and voices of people who have been silenced.

Race: Race is a term that categorizes people based on what you see (physical characteristics such as skin color, hair texture, facial features, and eye color), and these categories are then used to create hierarchies of value.

Race-based stereotype: A race-based stereotype is words, images, or actions that assume a group of people who share some characteristics also share certain attributes. Race-based stereotypes are hurtful, simplistic, dangerous, and unfair.

Racial justice: Racial justice means that on a systemic level all people are treated equally and fairly.

Racial prejudice: Racial prejudice is making a negative assumption about someone based on race, ethnicity, or skin color.

Racial slur: A racial slur is any mean or hurtful comment about someone based on race, ethnicity, culture, or skin color.

Racism: Racism is a combination of prejudice and power against people of color. It is a system that disadvantages anyone who is not white.

Reparations: Reparations is the practice of repairing and restoring something that has been stolen from someone, whether that be a person's history, rights and privileges, or dignity.

Transracial adoption: Transracial adoption means that a child of one race or ethnic group is adopted by a family of a different race or ethnic group.

White privilege: White privilege means that white people are given unearned benefits and advantages due to the color of their skin, and these same benefits and advantages are denied to people with non-white skin.

White supremacy: When people believe in white supremacy, they believe that white people are better than everyone else.

Media Suggestions for a Race-Wise Family

We hope that these books, movies, and television shows can serve your family as launching points for conversation and growth in understanding issues of race and ethnicity. This is not intended to be an exhaustive list but instead a place to start your search for resources to use with your children. Please note that not all these resources reflect a Christian point of view. Use discretion as you choose what to use in your own family.

General Guidelines for Using This Resource List

- Remember that the Holy Spirit is alive and working as you read, listen, or watch. So first ask the Holy Spirit to prepare your hearts and minds. Afterward ask the Spirit to guide your exploration of these issues and your interactions with others.
- Recognize that conversations about race and racism can be difficult. They often unearth buried memories that may be traumatic or shame filled. Have grace for

yourself and your children, and let your conversations be guided by hope for true healing.

- Come ready to learn and to be seen. Being able to explore and further develop our ethnic and racial identities often allows us to experience healing as we are seen for who we really are and accepted. However, these conversations can also reveal long-standing divisions in our churches, ministries, organizations, and families. Recognizing that you still have room to grow, allow division and conflict to be opportunities for learning.

Reflection Questions to Discuss with Your Children

- What stood out to you in this book or movie?
- What issues did people of color face in this book or movie?
- How did the main character(s) respond?
- Was this the right or wrong approach? Why?
- How would you respond in this situation?
- What did you learn about the issues we're reading about or seeing today?
- What questions do you have?

Toddler and Preschool (ages 1-4):

Picture Books

- *10 Gulab Jamuns: Counting with an Indian Sweet Treat* by Sandhya Acharya (Mascot Books, 2017)
- *Asian Adventures A–Z* by Yobe Qiu (Yobe Qiu, 2020)
- *Hair Love* by Matthew A. Cherry (Kokila, 2019)
- *How Are You?/¿Cómo estás?* by Angela Dominguez (Henry Holt, 2018)
- *If You're Going to a March* by Martha Freeman (Sterling Children's Books, 2018)

- *Love Gave: A Story of God's Greatest Gift* by Quina Aragon (Harvest House, 2021)
- *Love Made: A Story of God's Overflowing, Creative Heart* by Quina Aragon (Harvest House, 2019)
- *The Preschooler's Bible* by V. Gilbert Beers, 2nd ed. (David C Cook, 2012)
- *The Snowy Day* by Ezra Jack Keats (Viking, 2012)
- *Thread of Love* by Kabir Sehgal and Surishtha Sehgal (Beach Lane Books, 2018)
- *We're Different, We're the Same* by Bobbi Kates (Random House, 1992)
- *The Wheels on the Tuk Tuk* by Kabir Sehgal and Surishtha Sehgal (Beach Lane Books, 2016)
- *Woke Baby* by Mahogany L. Browne (Roaring Brook, 2018)

Early Elementary (ages 5–7)

Picture Books

- *The ABCs of Black History* by Rio Cortez (Workman, 2020)
- *All the Colors of the Earth* by Sheila Hamanaka (HarperCollins, 1999)
- *All the Colors We Are: The Story of How We Get Our Skin Color / Todos los colores de nuestra piel: La historia de por qué tenemos diferentes colores de piel* by Katie Kissinger (Redleaf, 2014)
- *Bee-Bim Bop!* by Linda Sue Park (Clarion, 2008)
- *The Celebration Place* by Dorena Williamson (IVP Kids, 2021)
- *ColorFull: Celebrating the Colors God Gave Us* by Dorena Williamson (B&H Kids, 2018)
- *The Colors of Us* by Karen Katz (Henry Holt, 1999)
- *Cora Cooks Pancit* by Dorina K. Lazo Gilmore (Shen's Books, 2009)

- *The Day You Begin* by Jacqueline Woodson (Nancy Paulsen Books, 2018)
- *Eyes That Kiss in the Corners* by Joanna Ho (Harper, 2021)
- *Fry Bread: A Native American Family Story* by Kevin Noble Maillard (Roaring Brook, 2019)
- *God Made Me AND You: Celebrating God's Design for Ethnic Diversity* by Shai Linne (New Growth Press, 2018)
- *God's Very Good Idea: A True Story About God's Delightfully Different Family* by Trillia J. Newbell (The Good Book Company, 2017)
- *GraceFull: Growing a Heart That Cares for Our Neighbors* by Dorena Williamson (B&H Kids, 2019)
- *Grandma's Purse* by Vanessa Brantley-Newton (Knopf, 2018)
- *Hair Like Mine* by LaTashia M. Perry (G Publishing, 2015)
- *Hidden Figures: The True Story of Four Black Women and the Space Race* by Margot Lee Shetterly (HarperCollins, 2018)
- *I Am Enough* by Grace Byers (Balzer + Bray, 2018)
- *I Love My Hair!* by Natasha Anastasia Tarpley (Little, Brown, 1997)
- *Islandborn* by Junot Díaz (Dial Books, 2018)
- *Josey Johnson's Hair and the Holy Spirit* by Esau McCaulley (IVP Kids, 2022)
- *A Kids Book About: Racism* by Jelani Memory (A Kids Book About, 2019)
- *Last Stop on Market Street* by Matt de la Peña (G. P. Putnam's Sons, 2015)
- *Laxmi's Mooch* by Shelly Anand (Kokila, 2021)
- *The Name Jar* by Yangsook Choi (Dragonfly Books, 2001)
- *The Paper Kingdom* by Helena Ku Rhee (Random House, 2020)

- *The Proudest Blue: A Story of Hijab and Family* by Ibtihaj Muhammad with S. K. Ali (Little, Brown, 2019)
- *Saturday* by Oge Mora (Little, Brown, 2019)
- *Shades of People* by Shelley Rotner and Sheila M. Kelly (Holiday House, 2010)
- *Skin Like Mine* by LaTashia M. Perry (G Publishing, 2016)
- *The Skin You Live In* by Michael Tyler (Chicago Children's Museum, 2005)
- *Sulwe* by Lupita Nyong'o (Penguin, 2021)
- *Tea Cakes for Tosh* by Kelly Starling Lyons (G. P. Putnam's Sons, 2012)
- *ThoughtFull: Discovering the Unique Gifts in Each of Us* by Dorena Williamson (B&H, 2018)
- *We Are Grateful: Otsaliheliga* by Traci Sorell (Charlesbridge, 2018)
- *When We Were Alone* by David A. Robertson (HighWater, 2016)
- *Where Are You From?* by Yamile Saied Méndez (Harper, 2019)

Chapter Books

- *The Story of…* Biography Series for New Readers by various authors (Rockridge Press, 2020–2021). This series of thirty-one books features the biographies of historical and contemporary figures, including Frida Kahlo, Malala Yousafzai, Nelson Mandela, Kamala Harris, Jackie Robinson, Simone Biles, Mahatma Gandhi, and Harriet Tubman.

Movies and Television Shows

Please note: While we appreciate and value the cultural messages in the following movies and shows, we encourage parents to do their own vetting to make sure they are comfortable with the content. You know your children best and, by doing this research beforehand, can discern whether any given film is appropriate for them.

- *Coco,* PG (Walt Disney Studios, 2017)
- *Encanto,* PG (Walt Disney Studios, 2021)
- *Hair Love,* G (Sony, 2019)
- *Liberty's Kids:* Season 1, Episode 37, "Born Free and Equal," TV-Y7 (PBS, April 1, 2003)
- *Mira, Royal Detective,* TV-Y7 (Disney Junior, 2020)
- *Moana,* PG (Walt Disney Studios, 2016)
- *Recess:* Season 1, Episode 4, "The Great Jungle Gym Standoff," TV-Y7 (ABC, September 20, 1997)

Late Elementary/Middle School (ages 8-12)

Picture Books

- *Freedom River* by Doreen Rappaport (Hyperion Book, 2000)
- *Not My Idea: A Book About Whiteness* by Anastasia Higginbotham (Dottir, 2018)
- *Separate Is Never Equal: Sylvia Mendez and Her Family's Fight for Desegregation* by Duncan Tonatiuh (Abrams, 2014)
- *Something Happened in Our Town: A Child's Story About Racial Injustice* by Marianne Celano, Marietta Collins, and Ann Hazzard (Magination, 2019)
- *Todos iguales: Un corrido de Lemon Grove / All Equal: A Ballad of Lemon Grove* by Christy Hale (Lee & Low, 2019)
- *Voice of Freedom: Fannie Lou Hamer: The Spirit of the Civil Rights Movement* by Carole Boston Weatherford (Candlewick, 2018)
- *Young Water Protectors: A Story About Standing Rock* by Aslan Tudor and Kelly Tudor (CreateSpace, 2018)

- *The Youngest Marcher: The Story of Audrey Faye Hendricks, a Young Civil Rights Activist* by Cynthia Levinson (Atheneum, 2017)

Graphic Novels/Memoirs

- *New Kid* by Jerry Craft (Quill Tree Books, 2019)
- *Stargazing* by Jen Wang (First Second, 2019)
- *Superman Smashes the Klan* by Gene Luen Yang (DC Comics, 2020)
- *When Stars Are Scattered* by Victoria Jamieson and Omar Mohamed (Dial Books, 2020)

Chapter Books

- *Brown Girl Dreaming* by Jacqueline Woodson (Nancy Paulsen Books, 2016)
- *Bud, Not Buddy* by Christopher Paul Curtis (Yearling, 2002)
- *Count Me In* by Varsha Bajaj (Puffin, 2020)
- *Creative God, Colorful Us* by Trillia J. Newbell (Moody, 2021)
- *Crossing the Wire* by Will Hobbs (HarperCollins, 2007)
- *Esperanza Rising* by Pam Muñoz Ryan (Scholastic, 2002)
- *Front Desk* by Kelly Yang (Arthur A. Levine, 2019)
- *Ghost Boys* by Jewell Parker Rhodes (Little, Brown, 2019)
- *A Good Kind of Trouble* by Lisa Moore Ramée (Balzer + Bray, 2020)
- *Harbor Me* by Jacqueline Woodson (Puffin, 2020)
- *A Long Walk to Water: Based on a True Story* by Linda Sue Park (HMH Books, 2011)
- *Pippa Park Raises Her Game* by Erin Yun (Fabled Films Press, 2021)
- *Project Mulberry* by Linda Sue Park (Clarion, 2017)
- *Roll of Thunder, Hear My Cry* by Mildred D. Taylor (Puffin, 2004)

- *The Story of Ruby Bridges* by Robert Coles (Scholastic, 2010)
- *The Watsons Go to Birmingham—1963* by Christopher Paul Curtis (Yearling, 1997)
- *What Lane?* by Torrey Maldonado (Nancy Paulsen Books, 2021)
- *Young, Gifted and Black: Meet 52 Black Heroes from Past and Present* by Jamia Wilson (Wide Eyed Editions, 2018)

Novel in Verse

- *Other Words for Home* by Jasmine Warga (Balzer + Bray, 2021)

Movies

- *Akeelah and the Bee*, PG (Lionsgate, 2006)
- *A Ballerina's Tale*, NR (Sundance Selects, 2015)
- *Spider-Man: Into the Spider-Verse*, PG (Sony, 2018)
- *Wadjda*, PG (Sony, 2012)

Teens (ages 13-18)

Books

- *All American Boys* by Jason Reynolds and Brendan Kiely (Atheneum/Caitlyn Dlouhy Books, 2017)
- *American Immigration: Our History, Our Stories* by Kathleen Krull (HarperCollins, 2020)
- *The Hate U Give* by Angie Thomas (Balzer + Bray, 2017)
- *If I Ever Get Out of Here* by Eric Gansworth (Arthur A. Levine, 2015)
- *It's Trevor Noah: Born a Crime: Stories from a South African Childhood* (Adapted for Young Readers) by Trevor Noah (Yearling, 2020)

- *Just Mercy: A True Story of the Fight for Justice* (Adapted for Young Adults) by Bryan Stevenson (Ember, 2019)
- *On the Come Up* by Angie Thomas (Balzer + Bray, 2019)
- *Piecing Me Together* by Renée Watson (Bloomsbury, 2018)
- *A Step from Heaven* by An Na (Front Street, 2001)
- The Sunlit Lands series by Matt Mikalatos (Wander, 2021)
- *This Is My America* by Kim Johnson (Random House, 2020)
- *This Side of Home* by Renée Watson (Bloomsbury, 2017)
- *Through My Eyes* by Ruby Bridges (Scholastic, 1999)
- *We Are Not Free* by Traci Chee (Clarion, 2020)
- *We Are Not from Here* by Jenny Torres Sanchez (Philomel, 2021)

Graphic Novels/Memoirs

- *Almost American Girl* by Robin Ha (Balzer + Bray, 2020)
- *American Born Chinese* by Gene Luen Yang (First Second, 2021)
- *They Called Us Enemy* by George Takei, Justin Eisinger, and Steven Scott (Top Shelf Productions, 2019)

Picture Books

- *A Wreath for Emmett Till* by Marilyn Nelson (Clarion, 2009)

Movies and Television Shows

Please note: While we appreciate the following shows and movies for tackling issues of race and ethnicity, we encourage parents to do their own vetting to make sure they are comfortable with the content. We have added the TV Parental Guidelines and MPAA ratings to help guide you, but ultimately parents will want to determine whether the content is appropriate for their families. Shows rated PG and TV-14 often involve themes that touch on mature topics such as sexuality, but we included the few here because of the authentic portrayal of race, ethnicity, and culture that can increase understanding and spark conversations between teens and parents. For more information on any of these titles, we recommend sites such as Common Sense Media so you can decide what is best for you and your children.

Movies

- *42*, PG-13 (Warner Bros., 2013)
- *Amazing Grace*, PG (Samuel Goldwyn, 2006)
- *Becoming*, PG (Netflix, 2020)
- *Belle*, PG (Fox Searchlight, 2013)
- *Black Panther*, PG-13 (Walt Disney Studios, 2018)
- *The Boy Who Harnessed the Wind*, TV-PG (Netflix, 2019)
- *Get Out*, R (Universal, 2017) Note: Despite the R rating, we recommend this film for older teens and young adults due to the powerful social commentary that Jordan Peele makes. The R rating is due to scary moments and some violence; it is considered a borderline horror movie, but the horror comes less from the limited violence and more from the challenging nature of the storyline.
- *Glory Road*, PG (Buena Vista, 2006)
- *The Hate U Give*, PG-13 (Twentieth Century Studios, 2018)
- *The Help*, PG-13 (Walt Disney Studios, 2011)
- *Hidden Figures*, PG (Twentieth Century Fox, 2016)
- *Hoop Dreams*, PG-13 (Fine Line Features, 1994)
- *Invictus*, PG-13 (Warner Bros., 2009)
- *Just Mercy*, PG-13 (Warner Bros., 2019)

- *Liyana,* NR (Abramorama, 2017)
- *McFarland, USA,* PG (Walt Disney Studios, 2015)
- *Million Dollar Arm,* PG (Walt Disney Studios, 2014)
- *Minari,* PG-13 (A24, 2020)
- *Remember the Titans,* PG (Buena Vista, 2000)
- *The Revolutionary Optimists,* NR (Shadow Distribution, 2013)
- *The Secret Life of Bees,* PG-13 (Fox Searchlight, 2008)
- *Selma,* PG-13 (Paramount, 2014)
- *Shang-Chi and the Legend of the Ten Rings,* PG-13 (Walt Disney Studios, 2021)
- *Smoke Signals,* PG-13 (Miramax, 1998)
- *To Kill a Mockingbird,* NR (Universal, 1962)

Television Shows

- *All American,* TV-14 (The CW, 2018)
- *Black-ish,* TV-PG (ABC, 2014)
- *Fresh Off the Boat,* TV-PG (ABC, 2015)
- *Friday Night Lights,* TV-14 (NBC, 2006)
- *Kim's Convenience,* TV-14 (Netflix, 2016)

Prayers for a Race-Wise Family

You can download a free version of the prayers included at the end of each posture in the book. Print them out and display them in your home in a highly visible place (such as on the refrigerator door or a bathroom mirror) and/or use them in your own devotional times. Visit wmbooks.com/racewiseextras to get a copy for yourself or to share with others.

Recommendations for Future Learning for Parents

The following is a brief list of other resources that have been fundamental in our own journey of becoming race-wise parents. We hope they can be helpful to you as well.

Books

- *Be the Bridge: Pursuing God's Heart for Racial Reconciliation* by Latasha Morrison (WaterBrook, 2019)
- *Between the World and Me* by Ta-Nehisi Coates (One World, 2015)
- *Beyond Colorblind: Redeeming Our Ethnic Journey* by Sarah Shin (IVP Books, 2017)
- *The Color of Compromise: The Truth About the American Church's Complicity in Racism* by Jemar Tisby (Zondervan, 2020)
- *The Gospel in Color Set: A Theology of Racial Reconciliation for Families* by Curtis A. Woods and Jarvis J. Williams (Patrol, 2018)

- *How to Fight Racism: Courageous Christianity and the Journey Toward Racial Justice* by Jemar Tisby (Zondervan, 2021)
- *I'm Still Here: Black Dignity in a World Made for Whiteness* by Austin Channing Brown (Convergent, 2018)
- *Just Mercy: A Story of Justice and Redemption* by Bryan Stevenson (One World, 2014)
- *Mixed Blessing: Embracing the Fullness of Your Multiethnic Identity* by Chandra Crane (IVP, 2020)
- *The Myth of Equality: Uncovering the Roots of Injustice and Privilege* by Ken Wytsma (IVP, 2019)
- *Prophetic Lament: A Call for Justice in Troubled Times* by Soong-Chan Rah (IVP, 2015)
- *Rediscipling the White Church: From Cheap Diversity to True Solidarity* by David W. Swanson (IVP, 2020)
- *Roadmap to Reconciliation 2.0: Moving Communities into Unity, Wholeness and Justice* by Brenda Salter McNeil (IVP, 2020)
- *Tears We Cannot Stop: A Sermon to White America* by Michael Eric Dyson (St. Martin's Griffin, 2021)

Online Resources

- Be the Bridge website, especially "16 Tips for White Bridge-Builders" (https://bethebridge.com/btb101), and Be the Bridge Facebook group, especially "10 Things Every Racial Bridge-Builder Should Know"
- Brownicity's "Let's Learn About" course for preschool and elementary-aged children (https://join.brownicity.com/courses/b-kids)

Notes

Introduction

1. The title of our book offers a nod to Andy Crouch, who coined the phrase *tech-wise* in his book *The Tech-Wise Family*.

Posture One: Valuing Multiethnicity

1. Dictionary.com, s.v. "ethnicity," www.dictionary.com /browse/ethnicity.
2. Richie Zweigenhaft, "Fortune 500 CEOs, 2000–2020: Still Male, Still White," The Society Pages, October 28, 2020, https://thesocietypages.org/specials/fortune-500 -ceos-2000-2020-still-male-still-white.
3. Bruce K. Waltke, *Genesis: A Commentary* (Grand Rapids, MI: Zondervan, 2001), 62.
4. "What Is Multiethnicity?," InterVarsity Multiethnic Ministries, https://mem.intervarsity.org/what -multiethnicity.

5. William H. Frey, "The US Will Become 'Minority White' in 2045, Census Projects," Brookings, March 14, 2018, www.brookings.edu/blog/the-avenue/2018/03/14/the-us-will-become-minority-white-in-2045-census-projects.

6. William H. Frey, "Less Than Half of US Children Under 15 Are White, Census Shows," Brookings, June 24, 2019, www.brookings.edu/research/less-than-half-of-us-children-under-15-are-white-census-shows.

7. Alex Vandermaas-Peeler et al., "Partisan Polarization Dominates Trump Era: Findings from the 2018 American Values Survey," PRRI, October 29, 2018, www.prri.org/research/partisan-polarization-dominates-trump-era-findings-from-the-2018-american-values-survey.

8. Jemar Tisby, quoted in Eugene Scott, "More Than Half of White Evangelicals Say America's Declining White Population Is a Negative Thing," *Washington Post*, July 18, 2018, www.washingtonpost.com/news/the-fix/wp/2018/07/18/more-than-half-of-white-evangelicals-say-americas-declining-white-population-is-a-negative-thing.

9. Dorina Lazo Gilmore-Young, "Global Glory Chasers: Traveling the World from the Comfort of Home," Dorina Lazo Gilmore-Young, April 29, 2021, https://dorinagilmore.com/global-glory-chasers-traveling-the-world-from-the-comfort-of-home.

Posture Two: Seeing Color

1. *American Heritage Dictionary*, s.v. "culture," https://ahdictionary.com/word/search.html?q=culture.

2. "QuickFacts: United States," United States Census Bureau, www.census.gov/quickfacts/fact/table/US/PST045219.

3. Theopulos, "The Hellenistic Widows," Fuller Theological Seminary, www.fuller.edu/next-faithful -step/resources/the-hellenistic-widows.

4. Theopulos, "The Hellenistic Widows." See Martin Hengel, "Judaism and Hellenism Revisited," in *Hellenism in the Land of Israel*, eds. John J. Collins and Gregory E. Sterling (Notre Dame, IN: University of Notre Dame Press, 2001); Young Lee Hertig, "Cross-Cultural Mediation: From Exclusion to Inclusion (Acts 6:1–7; also 5:33–42)," in *Mission in Acts: Ancient Narratives in Contemporary Context*, eds. Robert L. Gallagher and Paul Hertig (Maryknoll, NY: Orbis Books, 2004), 59–72.

5. James D. G. Dunn, *Beginning from Jerusalem* (Grand Rapids, MI: Eerdmans, 2009), 251.

6. Thanks to Sarah Shin for articulating this point more fully in her excellent book *Beyond Colorblind: Redeeming Our Ethnic Journey*. See chapter 8, "Responding to Crosscultural Conflict in Community," for a deeper dive into the issues that arose in this situation.

7. Madeleine Rogin, "What Is 'The Talk' White Parents Should Have with White Children?," Embrace Race, www.embracerace.org/resources/what-is-the-talk-white -parents-should-have-with-white-children.

8. In this book, we will use the phrase *people of color* to refer to those who are non-white, racially speaking.

9. Sarah Shin, *Beyond Colorblind: Redeeming Our Ethnic Journey* (Downers Grove, IL: IVP Books, 2017), 6.

10. David J. Kelly et al., "Three-Month-Olds, but Not Newborns, Prefer Own-Race Faces," Developmental Science 8, no. 6 (2005): F31–36, https://doi.org/10.1111 /j.1467-7687.2005.0434a.x.

Posture Three: Understanding a Biblical View of Racism

1. Beverly M. Pratt, Lindsay Hixson, and Nicholas A. Jones, "Measuring Race and Ethnicity Across the Decades: 1790–2010" United States Census Bureau, www.census.gov/data-tools/demo/race/MREAD _1790_2010.html.

2. Eric Jensen et al. "Measuring Racial and Ethnic Diversity for the 2020 Census," United States Census Bureau, August 14, 2021, www.census.gov/newsroom /blogs/random-samplings/2021/08/measuring-racial -ethnic-diversity-2020-census.html.

3. See David T. Wellman, *Portraits of White Racism* (New York: Cambridge University Press, 1977); Beverly Daniel Tatum, "Talking About Race, Learning About Racism: The Application of Racial Identity Development Theory in the Classroom," *Harvard Educational Review* 62, no. 1 (1992): 3.

4. "Brothers and Sisters to Us," United States Conference of Catholic Bishops, www.usccb.org/committees /african-american-affairs/brothers-and-sisters-us.

5. "Brothers and Sisters to Us."

6. Michelle Ami Reyes, "Justice, Restoration & Wholeness in the Kingdom of God," *The Better Samaritan,* March 12, 2021, www.christianitytoday.com/better-samaritan /2021/march/justice-restoration-wholeness-in -kingdom-of-god.html.

7. Adrian Pei, *The Minority Experience: Navigating Emotional and Organizational Realities* (Downers Grove, IL: IVP Books, 2018), 7.

8. "Real US History for Kids," Families Embracing Diversity, https://familiesembracingdiversity.com/real -us-history-for-kids.

9. Keyana Stevens, "5-Minute Film Festival: Talking

About Race and Stereotypes," Edutopia, April 10, 2015, www.edutopia.org/blog/5-minute-film-festival-talking -about-race-and-stereotypes.

10. See Daniel Hill's excellent book *White Awake* for a detailed description of many of these stages, and see appendix 5 in our book for other recommended resources to help you become a race-wise parent.

11. With thanks to Tod Bolsinger, author of *Tempered Resilience*, for his usage of this term.

Posture Four: Opening Our Hearts to Lament

1. Russell Falcon, "Atlanta Shootings Put Spotlight on Surging Anti-Asian Sentiment in America," KXAN, March 17, 2021, www.kxan.com/news/atlanta -shootings-put-spotlight-on-surging-anti-asian -sentiment-in-america.

2. Amir Vera and Jason Hanna, "Here's What We Know About the Metro Atlanta Spa Shootings That Left 8 Dead," CNN, March 19, 2021, www.cnn.com/2021/03 /16/us/metro-atlanta-spa-shootings-what-we-know /index.html.

3. Anti-Asian hate related to COVID-19 has been covered in a wide variety of news sources. These include but are not limited to Sabrina Tavernise and Richard A. Oppel Jr., "Spit On, Yelled At, Attacked: Chinese-Americans Fear for Their Safety," *New York Times*, last modified May 5, 2021, www.nytimes.com/2020/03/23 /us/chinese-coronavirus-racist-attacks.html; Russell Jeung, "Asian Americans Are Blamed by Some for COVID-19 Outbreak," interview by Steve Inskeep, NPR, March 27, 2020, www.npr.org/2020/03/27 /822383360/asian-americans-are-blamed-by-some-for -covid-19-outbreak.

4. See Stop AAPI Hate, https://stopaapihate.org, for more data related to anti-Asian hate crimes.

5. "What Is the Church's Role in Racial Reconciliation?," Barna, July 30, 2019, www.barna.com/research/racial -reconciliation.

6. "Empathy," *Psychology Today*, www.psychologytoday .com/us/basics/empathy.

7. Jamil Zaki, "Empathy Is on the Decline in This Country. A New Book Describes What We Can Do to Bring It Back," interview by Emma Seppälä, *Washington Post*, June 11, 2019, www.washingtonpost .com/lifestyle/2019/06/11/empathy-is-decline-this -country-new-book-describes-what-we-can-do-bring-it -back.

8. Belinda Bauman, *Brave Souls: Experiencing the Audacious Power of Empathy* (Downers Grove, IL: IVP Books, 2019), 9, 12.

9. Brian A. Primack et al., "Social Media Use and Perceived Social Isolation Among Young Adults in the U.S.," *American Journal of Preventive Medicine* 53, no. 1 (2017), https://doi.org/10.1016/j.amepre.2017 .01.010.

10. *Merriam-Webster*, s.v. "compassion," www.merriam -webster.com/dictionary/compassion.

11. "Understanding the Meaning of Compassion," Compassion International, www.compassion.com/child -development/meaning-of-compassion.

12. Andrew Williams, "Biblical Lament and Political Protest," *Cambridge Papers* 23, no. 1 (March 2014), www.jubilee-centre.org/cambridge-papers/biblical -lament-political-protest-andrew-williams.

13. Rebekah Eklund, *Jesus Wept: The Significance of Jesus' Laments in the New Testament* (London: Bloomsbury T&T Clark, 2015), 16–17.

14. Nijay Gupta, "Soong-Chan Rah Calls the American Church to Lament," Missio Alliance, October 19, 2015,

www.missioalliance.org/soong-chan-rah-calls-the
-american-church-to-lament.

15. Soong-Chan Rah, *Prophetic Lament: A Call for Justice
in Troubled Times* (Downers Grove, IL: IVP Books,
2015), 23.

16. Cornel West, *Race Matters* (Boston: Beacon, 2017), xxi.

17. Williams, "Biblical Lament and Political Protest."

18. Williams, "Biblical Lament and Political Protest."

19. Dan Allender, "The Hidden Hope in Lament," The
Allender Center, June 2, 2016, https://theallendercenter
.org/2016/06/hidden-hope-lament.

20. Williams, "Biblical Lament and Political Protest."

21. The term *snowflake* is derogatory slang implying that a
person has an inflated sense of uniqueness, has an
unwarranted sense of entitlement, or is overly
emotional, easily offended, and unable to deal with
opposing opinions. *Snowflake* gained popularity during
the 2016 presidential election, initially used by the right
to describe their political opponents on the left.
Throughout 2020 and 2021, many Asian Americans
were called snowflakes by conservatives recounting
experiences of anti-Asian racism.

22. For example, after Ahmaud Arbery was killed on
February 23, 2020, two competing narratives developed.
Initially many tried to bring up Arbery's criminal
history to argue that he was "a terrible person that just
deserved to die, like his death was justified." On the
other hand, it was discovered that the perpetrator,
Travis McMichael, used a racial epithet after fatally
shooting Arbery. Later, video evidence proved that
these men "chased, hunted down, and ultimately
executed" Arbery. See Cleve R. Wootson Jr. and
Michael Brice-Saddler, " 'This Was Supposed to Go
Away': The Battle to Shape How the World Viewed
Ahmaud Arbery's Killing," *Washington Post,* May 23,
2020, www.washingtonpost.com/national/this-was

-supposed-to-go-away-the-battle-to-shape-how-the
-world-viewed-ahmaud-arberys-killing/2020/05/22
/089916b8-98f6-11ea-89fd-28fb313d1886_story.html;
Brakkton Booker, "White Defendant Allegedly Used
Racial Slur After Killing Ahmaud Arbery," NPR,
June 4, 2020, www.npr.org/2020/06/04/869938461
/white-defendant-allegedly-used-racial-slur-after
-killing-ahmaud-arbery.

23. See, for example, Jessica Lee, "Background Check:
Investigating George Floyd's Criminal Record," Snopes,
June 12, 2020, www.snopes.com/news/2020/06/12
/george-floyd-criminal-record. Regarding George
Floyd's criminal history, Lee wrote, "The question of
past arrests often surfaces among people who want to
rationalize police officers' actions when Black men are
killed in custody."

24. Some Native American leaders and activists are
frustrated that conversations about stolen land are
limited to apologies without any mention of
reparations. Moreover, most folks don't know what
Native American land they live on. See Crystal
EchoHawk, "Stolen Land, Stolen Bodies, and Stolen
Stories," *Stanford Social Innovation Review*, February 25,
2021, https://ssir.org/articles/entry/stolen_land
_stolen_bodies_and_stolen_stories. EchoHawk argued
that "the largest narrative barrier facing Native peoples
is *invisibility* in the minds of the public, the media, the
education system, and popular culture: 78 percent of
Americans said they know little to nothing about Native
Americans."

25. See Miranda Bryant, "Allegations of Unwanted ICE
Hysterectomies Recall Grim Time in US History,"
Guardian, September 21, 2020, www.theguardian.com
/us-news/2020/sep/21/unwanted-hysterectomy
-allegations-ice-georgia-immigration.

26. See CT Editors, "John MacArthur's 'Statement on Social Justice' Is Aggravating Evangelicals," *Christianity Today*, September 12, 2018, www.christianitytoday.com /ct/podcasts/quick-to-listen/john-macarthur-statement -social-justice-gospel-thabiti.html.

27. Soong-Chan Rah, quoted in J. Todd Billings, "How Learning to Lament Can Help Fight Racism," *Relevant*, May 5, 2016, www.relevantmagazine.com/current/how -learning-lament-can-help-fight-racism.

Posture Five: Speaking Words of Love and Truth

1. See Lawrence A. Hirschfeld, "Seven Myths of Race and the Young Child," *Du Bois Review* 9, no. 1 (2012): 17–39, https://doi.org/10.1017/S1742058X12000033.

2. See Robin Kawakami, "I'm Asian American. When Will People Stop Seeing Me as a Forever Foreigner?," Today, March 24, 2021, www.today.com/tmrw/i-m-asian -american-when-will-people-stop-seeing-me-t212664.

3. See "Immigration," Gallup, https://news.gallup.com /poll/1660/immigration.aspx. See also Samantha Laine Perfas, Henry Gass, and Jessica Mendoza, "Why Do Americans Think More Immigration Means More Crime?," *Christian Science Monitor*, August 17, 2020, www.csmonitor.com/USA/Justice/2020/0817/Why-do -Americans-think-more-immigration-means-more -crime-audio.

4. On the racialization of crime, see Lincoln Quillian and Devah Pager, "Black Neighbors, Higher Crime? The Role of Racial Stereotypes in Evaluations of Neighborhood Crime," *American Journal of Sociology* 107, no. 3 (November 2001): 717–67, https://doi.org/10 .1086/338938; Elizabeth Sun, "The Dangerous Racialization of Crime in U.S. News Media," Center for

American Progress, August 29, 2018, www
.americanprogress.org/issues/criminal-justice/news
/2018/08/29/455313/dangerous-racialization-crime
-u-s-news-media.

5. See "What Does the Bible Say About Stereotypes?," Got
   Questions, www.gotquestions.org/Bible-stereotypes
   .html.

6. *American Heritage Dictionary*, s.v. "prejudice," https://
   ahdictionary.com/word/search.html?q=prejudice.

7. J. Daniel Hays, *From Every People and Nation: A
   Biblical Theology of Race* (Downers Grove, IL:
   InterVarsity Press, 2003), 71.

Posture Six: Responding to Current Events

1. Rhea Boyd, "How to Talk to Your Children About
   Protests and Racism," interview by Sandee LaMotte,
   CNN, June 2, 2020, www.cnn.com/2020/06/01/health
   /protests-racism-talk-to-children-wellness/index.html.

2. See Grace Panetta, "Conservative Media Described
   Immigration as an 'Invasion' Hundreds of Times Before
   the El Paso Shooter Echoed the Same Language,"
   Business Insider, August 12, 2019, www.businessinsider
   .com/conservative-media-often-called-immigration
   -invasion-before-el-paso-2019-8.

3. Karl Barth, quoted in "Barth in Retirement," *Time*,
   May 31, 1963, http://content.time.com/time
   /subscriber/article/0,33009,896838,00.html.

4. Joe Carter, "How Should Christians Think About 'the
   News'?," The Ethics & Religious Liberty Commission of
   the Southern Baptist Convention, January 25, 2018,
   https://erlc.com/resource-library/articles/how-should
   -christians-think-about-the-news.

5. Joe Carter, "Discernment in the Age of Instant News,"
   interview by Traci Devette Griggs, NC Family Policy

Council, April 9, 2020, www.ncfamily.org/discernment
-in-the-age-of-instant-news.

6. Ken Wytsma, *The Myth of Equality: Uncovering the Roots of Injustice and Privilege*, rev. ed. (Downers Grove, IL: InterVarsity, 2019), 157.

7. Bill Chappell and Richard Gonzales, "Brandt Jean's Act of Grace Toward His Brother's Killer Sparks a Debate over Forgiving," NPR, October 3, 2019, www.npr.org /2019/10/03/766866875/brandt-jeans-act-of-grace -toward-his-brother-s-killer-sparks-a-debate-over-forgi.

8. Allison Jean, quoted in "Botham Jean's Parents Speak to His Congregation, Father Says, 'I Would Like to Be Amber's Friend at Some Point,' " NBC DFW, October 2, 2019, www.nbcdfw.com/news/local/botham-jeans -parents-church-guygers-sentencing-father-says-i-would -like-ambers-friend/273456.

9. Dorena Williamson, "Botham Jean's Brother's Offer of Forgiveness Went Viral. His Mother's Calls for Justice Should Too," *Christianity Today*, October 4, 2019, www .christianitytoday.com/ct/2019/october-web-only /botham-jean-forgiveness-amber-guyger.html.

10. "Talking to Kids About Racism and Violence," Child Mind Institute, https://childmind.org/article/racism -and-violence-how-to-help-kids-handle-the-news.

11. Kenya Hameed, quoted in "Talking to Kids."

12. George Schroeder, "Seminary Presidents Reaffirm BFM, Declare CRT Incompatible," Baptist Press, November 30, 2020, www.baptistpress.com/resource -library/news/seminary-presidents-reaffirm-bfm -declare-crt-incompatible.

13. See, for example, Owen Strachan's sermon "What Are the Major Claims of Wokeness?," video, 1:03:12, October 5, 2020, www.youtube.com/watch?v=7BvWsCnRSxk&list= PLO3HHien0oFWA733Fms4nKNvO5jG52h8N.

14. See John Onwuchekwa, "4 Reasons We Left the SBC," The Front Porch, July 9, 2020, https://thefrontporch

.org/2020/07/4-reasons-we-left-the-sbc; Charlie Dates, " 'We Out': Charlie Dates on Why His Church Is Leaving the SBC over Rejection of Critical Race Theory," Religion News Service, December 18, 2020, https://religionnews.com/2020/12/18/we-out-charlie -dates-on-why-his-church-is-leaving-the-sbc-over -rejection-of-critical-race-theory.

15. Patricia Raybon, "Will We Judge Young Looters or Learn to Love Them?," (in)courage, July 8, 2020, www .incourage.me/2020/07/will-we-judge-young-looters -or-love-them-2.html.

16. Robin Terry Brown, quoted in Caroline Bologna, "How to Teach Kids Media Literacy," Huffington Post, November 12, 2020, www.huffpost.com/entry/parents -teach-kids-media-literacy_l_5fab43e3c5b6ed84597c3fc4.

17. Terry Brown, quoted in Bologna, "How to Teach Kids."

Posture Seven: Addressing Privilege

1. Peggy McIntosh, "White Privilege: Unpacking the Invisible Knapsack," *Peace and Freedom*, July–August 1989, 10–12, https://psychology.umbc.edu/files/2016 /10/White-Privilege_McIntosh-1989.pdf.

2. Brandon Griggs, "Living While Black," CNN, December 28, 2018, www.cnn.com/2018/12/20/us /living-while-black-police-calls-trnd/index.html.

3. Cory Collins, "What Is White Privilege, Really?," *Learning for Justice*, Fall 2018, www.learningforjustice .org/magazine/fall-2018/what-is-white-privilege-really.

4. US Declaration of Independence, www.archives.gov /founding-docs/declaration-transcript.

5. US Const. art. 1, § 2, www.archives.gov/founding-docs /constitution-transcript.

6. Mark Charles and Soong-Chan Rah, *Unsettling Truths:*

The Ongoing, Dehumanizing Legacy of the Doctrine of Discovery (Downers Grove, IL: InterVarsity, 2019), 83.

7. "Black Practicing Christians Are Twice as Likely as Their White Peers to See a Race Problem," Barna, June 17, 2020, www.barna.com/research/problems-solutions -racism.

8. See, for example, Andrew Lee's "Voices with Ed Stetzer: Standing Between White Privilege and Black Disprivilege: An Asian American Perspective," *Church Leaders,* November 4, 2020, https://churchleaders.com /voices/exchange/409465-voices-with-ed-stetzer -standing-between-white-privilege-and-black -disprivilege-an-asian-american-perspective.html. Lee argued, "As an Asian American, I need to continue to repent of my own learned prejudices and support the idea that Black Lives Matter. I need to voice my objection to Black Disprivilege and see each person as an individual, not a race. Their struggle is also my struggle as a person of color."

9. Brett Arends, "Black Children Are More Likely to Be Disciplined Than White Kids for the Same Behavior," Market Watch, October 16, 2019, www.marketwatch .com/story/black-children-are-more-likely-to-be -disciplined-than-white-kids-for-the-same-behavior -2019-10-16.

10. *2015–16 Civil Rights Data Collection: School Climate and Safety* (US Department of Education Office for Civil Rights, April 2018), 13, www2.ed.gov/about /offices/list/ocr/docs/school-climate-and-safety.pdf; see also Eliza Shapiro, "Students of Color Are More Likely to Be Arrested in School. That May Change," *New York Times,* June 20, 2019, www.nytimes.com /2019/06/20/nyregion/new-york-schools-police.html.

11. Brett Arends, "Black Children Are More Likely to Be Disciplined."

12. *Holman Bible Dictionary*, s.v. "stewardship," www
    .studylight.org/dictionaries/eng/hbd/s/stewardship
    .html.

13. Duke Kwon and Gregory Thompson, *Reparations: A
    Christian Call for Repentance & Repair* (Brazos Press,
    2021), 17.

14. Anna Faircloth Feingold, "Recovering White Identity,"
    Made for Pax, www.madeforpax.org/cultural-identity
    /material#anna-faircloth-feingold.

15. Michelle Reyes, "Let's Talk About White Privilege &
    Slavery," Asian American Christian Collaborative,
    June 22, 2020, www.asianamericanchristiancollaborative
    .com/article/lets-talk-about-white-privilege-and
    -slavery.

16. We highly recommend listening to the *New York Times*
    podcast *Nice White Parents* for an illuminating look at
    how well-intentioned parents who are trying to help
    their communities can actually end up fortifying white
    supremacy despite their best efforts.

17. "Race Matters: A Story About White Privilege," Raising
    Race Conscious Children, July 18, 2017, www
    .raceconscious.org/2017/07/race-matters-story-white
    -privilege.

18. Allison Holker, "White Privilege Is Real," Instagram
    video, June 2, 2020, www.instagram.com/tv
    /CA8xzw4BmMl/?utm_source=ig_embed.

19. Cut, "Black Parents Explain How to Deal with the
    Police," video, 5:30, February 6, 2017, www.youtube
    .com/watch?app=desktop&v=coryt8IZ-DE&feature=
    youtu.be.

Posture Eight: Assessing Your Biases

1. "Understanding Implicit Bias," Kirwan Institute for the
   Study of Race and Ethnicity, May 29, 2012, https://

kirwaninstitute.osu.edu/article/understanding-implicit
-bias.

2. "Understanding Implicit Bias."

3. "Preliminary Information," Project Implicit, https://
implicit.harvard.edu/implicit/takeatest.html.

4. E. Randolph Richards and Brandon J. O'Brien,
*Misreading Scripture with Western Eyes: Removing
Cultural Blinders to Better Understand the Bible*
(Downers Grove, IL: IVP Books, 2012), 16–17, emphasis
added.

5. Esau McCaulley, *Reading While Black: African
American Biblical Interpretation as an Exercise in Hope*
(Downers Grove, IL: IVP Academic, 2020), 101–2.

6. Tod Bolsinger, *Tempered Resilience: How Leaders Are
Formed in the Crucible of Change* (Downers Grove, IL:
InterVarsity, 2020).

7. Po Bronson and Ashley Merryman, *NurtureShock: New
Thinking About Children* (New York: Twelve, 2009), 60.

8. Martin Luther King Jr., interview, *Meet the Press*, NBC,
April 17, 1960, http://okra.stanford.edu/transcription
/document_images/Vol05Scans/17Apr1960
_InterviewonMeetthePress.pdf.

9. Michael O. Emerson, "Released! New 2020 Statistics on
Multiracial Churches," Multiethnic.Church, January 8,
2020, https://multiethnic.church/released-new-2020
-statistics-on-multiracial-churches.

10. Rebeca Ansar, "Here's a Riddle That Might Expose
Your Blind Spot," Medium, January 14, 2020, https://
medium.com/an-amygdala/heres-a-riddle-that-might
-expose-your-blind-spot-fc2902b4434d.

11. "Implicit Bias," UCLA Equity, Diversity & Inclusion,
https://equity.ucla.edu/know/implicit-bias.

12. Jennifer L. Eberhardt, "How Racial Bias Works—and
How to Disrupt It," TED, June 2020, www.ted.com
/talks/jennifer_l_eberhardt_how_racial_bias_works
_and_how_to_disrupt_it/up-next?language=en.

Posture Nine: Journeying Toward Racial Healing

1. Jacob Blake, quoted in Denise Lockwood, "In Kenosha, a Complicated Conversation Must Go On," CNN, January 19, 2021, www.cnn.com/2021/01/19/opinions /jacob-blake-shooting-kenosha-impact-lockwood/index .html.

2. "Racial Trauma," Mental Health America, www .mhanational.org/racial-trauma.

3. Ansley Booker, quoted in Jennifer Falk, "Mercer Offers Sessions for Students to Discuss Racial Trauma, Social Unrest," Mercer University, June 3, 2020, https://den .mercer.edu/mercer-offers-sessions-for-students-to -discuss-racial-trauma-social-unrest.

4. Sheila Wise Rowe, *Healing Racial Trauma: The Road to Resilience* (Downers Grove, IL: InterVarsity, 2020), 10.

5. "W. K. Kellogg Foundation Announces 14 Truth, Racial Healing & Transformation Engagements Throughout the United States," W. K. Kellogg Foundation, June 28, 2017, www.wkkf.org/news-and-media/article/2017/06 /wkkf-announces-14-truth-racial-healing-and -transformation-engagements-throughout-the-united -states.

6. Lexico, s.v. "safe space," www.lexico.com/en/definition /safe_space.

7. Michelle Reyes, "Finding Safe Spaces in the Midst of Racism," (in)courage, April 17 2020, www.incourage.me /2020/04/finding-safe-spaces-in-the-midst-of-racism .html; see also 1 Samuel 18–19; 21–24; 26–27; 1 Kings 19; Matthew 26.

8. Reyes, "Finding Safe Spaces."

9. Reyes, "Finding Safe Spaces"; see also 1 Peter 5:7.

10. Reyes, "Finding Safe Spaces."

11. Reyes, "Finding Safe Spaces."

12. Sheila Wise Rowe, *Healing Racial Trauma: The Road to Resilience* (Downers Grove, IL: InterVarsity, 2020), 4.

13. Rowe, *Healing Racial Trauma,* 143.

14. Sheila Wise Rowe, "Healing Racial Trauma," interview by Jamie D. Aten, *Psychology Today,* May 25, 2020, www.psychologytoday.com/us/blog/hope-resilience /202005/healing-racial-trauma.

15. Michelle Reyes, *Courageous Joy: Delight in God Through Every Season* (Revell, 2021): 183–84.

16. Reyes, *Courageous Joy.*

17. Reyes, *Courageous Joy.*

18. Martin Luther King Jr., "Nonviolence and Racial Justice," *Christian Century,* February 6, 1957, https:// kinginstitute.stanford.edu/king-papers/documents /nonviolence-and-racial-justice; Rowe, *Healing Racial Trauma,* 153.

19. "HILI Resource: Helping Children of Color Heal from Collective Trauma," UNITY, May 14, 2021, https:// unityinc.org/native-youth/hili-resource-helping -children-of-color-heal-from-collective-trauma.

Posture Ten: Raising Kingdom-Minded Children

1. In my (Helen's) time there, the re:generation Forum provided a context where we often talked about these cultural spheres.

2. David Swanson, personal communication with author.

3. C. S. Lewis, *The Lion, the Witch and the Wardrobe* (London: HarperCollins Children's Books, 2015), 75.

About the Authors

Helen Lee is the director of product innovation at InterVarsity Press, where she previously served as a marketing director and an acquisitions editor. An award-winning writer, she has frequently covered issues of race, ethnicity, and identity, including her seminal articles on Asian American Christianity that appeared in *Christianity Today* in 1996 ("Silent Exodus") and 2014 ("Silent No More"). Helen is a frequent conference speaker and has contributed to or authored a number of books, devotionals, and Bibles, including *Growing Healthy Asian American Churches* and *The Missional Mom*. She is also a serial entrepreneur/intrapreneur, founding or cofounding organizations such as Redbud Writers Guild, Ink Creative Collective, and Best Christian Workplaces Institute. Helen also serves as the executive producer of *The Disrupters* podcast, *The Every Voice Now Podcast*, and *Get in The Word with Truth's Table* podcast. She and her husband, Brian, have three sons and one mini-bernedoodle, and they live in Chicagoland. When she is not caring for family or working, she loves bird-watching, baking bread, and chipping away at middle-grade fiction. You can follow her on social media @helenleebooks and find out more about her at helenleebooks.com.

Michelle Ami Reyes, PhD, is the vice president of the Asian American Christian Collaborative, the scholar in residence at Hope Community Church, and the author of *Becoming All Things: How Small Changes Lead to Lasting Connections Across Cultures*. She has contributed chapters to several books, including *The Jesus I Wish I Knew in High School* and *Take Heart: 100 Devotions to Seeing God When Life's Not Okay*. She serves on the board for the Redbud Writers Guild, is a writing fellow at Missio Alliance, and is a regular contributor for (in)courage and Think Christian. Her writing on faith and culture can be found in many other publications, including *Christianity Today*, Patheos, and *Faithfully Magazine*. She lives in Austin, Texas, with her pastor husband and two amazing kids. You can connect with her and her work at michelleamireyes.com.